Environmental Learning for Classroom and Assembly at KS1 and KS2

T0084473

In *Environmental Learning for Classroom and Assembly at KS1 and KS2*, the highly successful and popular author Mal Leicester teams up with the conservationist Denise Taylor to teach children about wildlife and environmental conservation through the art of storytelling. Reflecting the child's world, the book works outwards from home to garden to neighbourhood to the countryside and seaside and to the planet as a whole. At each level, appreciating, conserving and enhancing our environment is considered.

The authors follow the tried and tested format of *Stories for Classroom and Assembly* and *Stories for Circle Time and Assembly*. Each of the eight chapters includes an original themed story and is packed with lesson plans and cross-curriculum learning activities designed to save teachers valuable time. Leicester and Taylor combine the wonder of storytelling with topical environmental issues, covering plants, creatures and the planet. The book covers the full range of conservation, protection and enhancement themes, concepts and values whilst developing the following skills:

- literacy (including oracy)
- numeracy
- knowledge of the natural world
- imaginative development
- creative expression.

Making a highly topical subject accessible to children, this beautifully illustrated resource offers teachers assembly ideas, lesson plans and art activities all in one book.

Mal Leicester is Professor Emeritus at Nottingham University, based in the School of Education.

Denise Taylor is an entrepreneur and conservationist whose primary interests are in education and learning in wildlife conservation.

Environmental Learning for Classroom and Assembly at KS1 and KS2

Stories about the natural world

Mal Leicester and Denise Taylor

Routledge
Taylor & Francis Group

LONDON AND NEW YORK

First published 2009
by Routledge
2 Park Square, Milton Park, Abingdon, Oxon OX14 4RN

Simultaneously published in the USA and Canada
by Routledge
270 Madison Avenue, New York, NY 10016

Routledge is an imprint of the Taylor & Francis Group, an informa business

Typeset in Bembo by
RefineCatch Limited, Bungay, Suffolk
Printed and bound in Great Britain by
the MPG Books Group in the UK

British Library Cataloguing in Publication Data
A catalogue record for this book is available from the British Library

Library of Congress Cataloging-in-Publication Data
Leicester, Mal.
   Environmental learning for classroom and assembly at KS1 and KS2 : stories
about the natural world / Mal Leicester and Denise Taylor.
       p. cm.
   1. Science—Study and teaching (Elementary)—Great Britain. 2. Environmental
education—Activity programs—Great Britain. 3. Storytelling. I. Taylor, Denise.
II. Title.
   LB1585.5.G7L45   2009
   372.35'7044—dc22   2008040854

ISBN 10: 0–415–48461–8 (hbk)
ISBN 10: 0–415–46707–1 (pbk)
ISBN 10: 0–203–88040–4 (ebk)

ISBN 13: 978–0–415–48461–9 (hbk)
ISBN 13: 978–0–415–46707–0 (pbk)
ISBN 13: 978–0–203–88040–1 (ebk)

Contents

Introduction

Stories, nature and the environment

In this book we combine the power of story with the magic of nature as a way into environmental education. Writers of stories and poetry often use the beauty, the enchantment and the sheer power of nature to deepen their descriptions and to highlight their themes. Indeed, much vivid writing is a tribute to the natural world, and images are captured in words to be recreated in our minds. For these reasons our stories focus on significant aspects of the natural environment to enhance the children's appreciation of our beautiful planet.

Used with flexibility, the material is appropriate for Key Stages 1 and 2, providing well planned teaching sessions, lovely illustrations and environmental learning activities with photocopiable resources. The stories reflect our multicultural world and embody environmental themes and values which are also used to plan for an associated school assembly.

Story and the curriculum

Storytelling has always been a powerful and basic human activity. In all civilisations and cultures, both the activity of storytelling and significant, individual stories have been passed down the generations. This is because long before the printed word was available, story was the means by which people attempted to make sense of their own experiences of the world, to communicate that understanding and to achieve a collective wisdom through passing on accumulated knowledge and values in a memorable and accessible way.

Stories both educate and entertain. We learn from them and the learning is fun. Because learning from stories is enjoyable, children simultaneously learn to love learning. Because children feel the power of story, to make use of stories in the classroom makes sound educational sense.

The stories in this book focus on our fragile earth – developing the children's appreciation of the wonders of nature, their understanding of the natural world and their commitment to environmental values.

Environmental education

Most modern children are interested in and concerned about their planet – the fragile earth. Many of them have seen documentaries such as *Planet Earth* and want to know more. It is important that children appreciate the life-enhancing wonders of the natural world, and their place as a part of nature. This vast and diverse topic incorporates the habitats and ecosystems of creatures and plants, biodiversity and endangered species, and an overview of planet earth – its water, air, land, flora and fauna. Environmental education aims to foster appreciation of the natural world, and develop understanding of the fragility of aspects of our planet, and what we can do to mitigate environmental problems. Thus, through environmental education the children learn to become good citizens of planet earth.

Environmental concerns are becoming increasingly important and will be even more so in the future, when the present generation have grown up. It is correspondingly important to begin environmental education at an early age. Such education will be rooted in a child's natural wonder at the natural world, encouraging appreciation and curiosity about the environment and our own interdependence with it. This should encourage a growing commitment to caring about the environment – *protecting, conserving and enhancing* our fragile planet – together with a developing understanding of what contributions the children can make to the green agenda.

Some key environmental concepts/words are as follows:

Biodiversity – the biological diversity (variety) of the plants and animals in the natural world
Ecosystem – a community of organisms (living things) and their environment.
Fauna – all forms of animal life (of a region or of Earth) as distinct from plant life.
Flora – all forms of vegetable life (of a region or of Earth) as distinct from animal life.
Habitat – the normal abode or locality of an animal or plant.
Species – a group of closely connected, mutually fertile individuals, which have characteristics in common.

How to use this book

Eight original, themed stories introduce chapters which focus on different aspects of our fragile earth – developing the children's appreciation of the wonders of nature, their understanding of the natural world and their commitment to environmental values. The stories widen out from the children's immediate environment (their homes and gardens) to an exploration of their neighbourhood. Subsequent chapters explore countryside and seaside environments, growing yet wider to include countries far away. Finally, farthest out as it were, Chapter 8 discusses global issues. Every chapter is concerned with *protecting, conserving and enhancing* the environment. Several optional learning activities are also suggested to provide material for further classroom work.

The environmental themes of each chapter readily lend themselves to national curriculum goals across the entire curriculum. They are a natural way into learning in both science and the arts. Each of the eight chapters is the focus for a teaching session with a story, some points for discussion and follow-up educational activities. Although approximate times are suggested for these activities, you should set a pace which suits you and your class. The intention is to save you time by providing good learning material for classroom work and for the school assembly. It would be useful before starting the activities in the book to arrange a bulk library loan. This can be used in conjunction with the school library and the IT suite, particularly for research activities for the older children.

Having introduced the theme of the story you can tell or read it perhaps with the children sitting in a circle. Deal with "difficult" vocabulary in your usual way which will sometimes mean explaining words as you come to them. You can select or add to the suggested activities and some of the optional activities are for use in follow-up lessons. You may also wish to use some of the classroom activity partly as preparation for the relevant assembly. Suggested poems and songs are given, taken from commonly used texts, but you will not find it difficult to find others which are relevant to the themes. It is an educative task to encourage the children themselves to make this selection.

You can link some of the material with other topics or projects. For example, some of the learning activities would be useful in natural history projects or with neighbourhood or seaside topics. There are activities and associated resources relevant to literacy work, to science, art, design and technology, religious education and geography. Moreover, the values aspects of the material are part of social, moral, multi-cultural and political education and much of it is appropriate to Citizenship.

The material is intended for use at Key Stages 1 and 2. Since this includes a relatively wide age range (4 to 11 years) you should use the material at the developmental level appropriate for your children. For example, younger children would enjoy making a rock pool after the story in Chapter 6 while older children will be able to write their own associated stories and poems and may even take a turn reading part of the theme story in the classroom or assembly.

Finally, as an appendix, we have provided a useful Environmental Education resource list, including books (fiction and non fiction), relevant organisations and websites. The internet has masses of excellent, relevant material. When you have used all eight chapters of the book, the Resource List will help you with your continuing environmental education.

CHAPTER 1

My Home is an Ecosystem

Theme One: My Home is an Ecosystem

In this chapter we explore the wonder of the natural world in our homes and gardens, and consider some of the creatures who share our living spaces, and how they survive.

In today's information society we have become used to seeing images of exotic creatures in far flung places, and we often think of the "natural world" as something that is far away from us. It is easy to overlook the fact that nature is all around us. There are lots of fascinating creatures that share our homes and gardens with us. This and the next chapter will encourage children to understand, appreciate, value and protect and conserve the flora and fauna right on their own doorstep and in their own back gardens.

Environmental Values

- Appreciation: Appreciation of the flora and fauna at home.
- Conservation: Conserving creatures in the home environment.
- Protection and enhancement: Valuing biodiversity in the home environment.

A Suggested Lesson Plan

1 **Introduce the theme**

How can we learn to understand and appreciate nature in and around our own homes?

2 **Vocabulary**

The teacher ensures that the children understand the words given.

3 The story

The teacher shows the illustration and reads the story.

4 Talking about the story

The teacher uses some of the questions and discussion points given, stimulating the children to talk about the story/theme.

5 Learning activities

The story activities encourage listening and discussion skills. Follow-up activities introduce environmental appreciation and understanding of the natural world in a home environment context. For environmental education, these activities encourage environmental values (e.g. appreciation/respect for the natural world), environmental concepts (e.g. biodiversity), and good environmental behaviour. In terms of personal development they also encourage listening skills, self-confidence and understanding the differences of others (by others we mean different species as well as people from other races, cultures or religions who might be different from ourselves).

1 INTRODUCE THE THEME

- Children are aware of the conservation issues affecting endangered species such as tigers, whales, pandas, turtles, etc., and may be aware of the ecosystems they live in. But in every home there are mini ecosystems to be explored. How many creatures share our living spaces – the home, garden, street and neighbourhood?
- Which creatures share our living spaces?
- How do they interact with us, each other and with other species?
- What do we mean by biodiversity? Why do we value it?
- Understanding family groups in other species.
- Understanding the basic principles of life-cycles, food chains, and predator/prey relationships.
- How can we develop tolerance of others?
- How can we learn to confront our fears?

2 VOCABULARY

Story vocabulary

Shrieked	–	*high-pitched scream*
Dashing	–	*moving fast*
Patiently	–	*able to wait*
Pretend	–	*to make believe*
Mottled	–	*marked with smears of colour*
Abdomen	–	*stomach or lower body*
Scuttled	–	*scurried along*
Bolted	–	*ran fast*
Funnel	–	*a tube or tube-like structure*
Retrieved	–	*found and brought back*
Spiderling	–	*a baby spider*

Associated environmental vocabulary

Predator/prey relationship	–	*the relationship between animals that hunt and those that are hunted*
Micro ecosystem	–	*a small or mini ecosystem*
Food chain	–	*the process of living on a smaller or weaker animal or plant in an ongoing chain*

Continued . . .

Lottie and Lily Longlegs

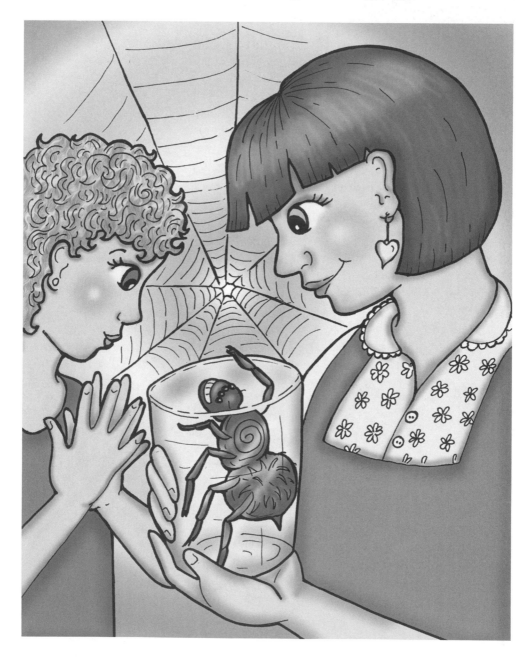

Lottie and Lily Longlegs

Lottie was tidying her bedroom, and bent down to move a small pile of magazines from underneath her bed. Suddenly a spider darted out, and ran towards Lottie. She shrieked, dropped the magazines, and leapt onto her bed.

"Mum, Mum. Come quick!" she yelled at the top of her lungs.

Lottie's Mum suddenly appeared at the door, out of breath from dashing up the stairs, to find out what all the fuss was about.

"There! It's over there." Lottie pointed to the bookcase. "It's gone under there."

"What has, Lottie? What's gone under there?" her Mum asked.

"A spider. It was big and fat and huge. And hairy. It's horrible and yucky. You have to get rid of it."

Lottie's Mum smiled patiently. "Lottie, calm down. It's only a tiny spider. You're much bigger than she is and she can't hurt you," she said. "Stay there while I go and fetch a glass."

Lottie stayed on her bed, watching the bookcase for any sign of movement. Soon her Mum reappeared carrying a glass and a piece of white card.

"It's OK, sweetheart. We'll just collect her up into this glass and then put her out in the garden."

"But how do you know it's a girl?" asked Lottie.

"I don't, but we can pretend it's a girl. Shall we give her a name?"

Lottie wasn't too sure this was a good idea. She was frightened of spiders, but she agreed anyway. "OK," she said, "we could call her Lily Longlegs."

"OK. Lily Longlegs it is. Come on, Lily, let's move you outside," said her Mum.

Carefully placing the glass over the spider, and then sliding the piece of card underneath, Lottie's Mum was able to capture Lily without harming her. Once Lottie realised that Lily couldn't escape so easily, she stood closer so that she could peer into the glass. The spider had two parts to its body. The front part, which had all eight legs attached to it, was the biggest part. The smaller part of the spider's body was brown with a pretty, mottled yellow pattern.

"The smaller part is its abdomen," said Lottie's Mum.

"Look Mum, one of her front legs is shorter than the others," said Lottie.

"Oh yes, so it is. But she seems OK. Let's go and put her out in the garden."

They went out into the front garden and very gently, Lottie's Mum lowered the glass, removed the cardboard and released the spider into the grass. She scuttled off quickly and was soon lost among the blades of grass and bright summer flowers.

Later that evening as they were all watching television, and just before her bedtime, Lottie's eye was caught by a quick movement by the side of the sofa. Suddenly, a large spider bolted out from under the sofa, and ran across the carpet towards the fireplace. Lottie again shrieked, and pulled her feet off the floor. The spider managed to reach the corner of the fireplace, and sat still for a while. Lottie's Mum went into the kitchen and for the second time came back with a glass and a piece of white card. They repeated the exercise of carefully capturing the spider in the glass, before putting it outside in the garden.

"Oooh, look Mum," said Lottie. "This one's also got a shorter front leg. Do you think it could be Lily?"

"It could be," said her Mum. "It seems a shame to put her back outside again in the cold. And spiders do help to get rid of the flies. Why don't we let her stay this time?"

"Oh, no," said Lottie. "You have to put her outside. She might crawl on me in the night, and I wouldn't like that." Lottie shivered at the thought of a spider crawling on her.

Her mother took the spider outside and let it go at the bottom of the garden.

The next morning Lottie was still sleepy. She'd dreamt about Lily Longlegs who was very sad and cold outside in the garden, and sat on her windowsill wanting to be let back in where it was safe and warm. Lottie sat up, stretched and yawned, and just as she was about to get out of bed she heard her Mum calling her from the bathroom.

"Lottie. Come quick. I think Lily Longlegs is back again."

Lottie rushed into the bathroom and sure enough, there was a large spider in the bath which seemed to have one front leg a lot shorter than all the others.

"What do you think we should do?" asked her Mum. "She seems very determined to keep coming back into the house. Are you sure we should put her outside?"

Despite her dream, Lottie still didn't much care for having big, hairy spiders in the house, and so the spider was put out into the garden again.

For the next three days, the spider kept appearing back in the house and each time Lottie's Mum gathered it up into the glass and put it back outside in the garden. Then the spider was no longer seen in the house. For a little while Lottie missed seeing Lily, she was getting so used to her coming into the house, but after a while she soon forgot about the spider.

A week later Lottie was playing in her bedroom when, out of the corner of her eye, she spotted a large, silky web in the window frame with a funnel in the middle of it. At the edge of the funnel sat a large, brown spider with one front leg shorter than all the others.

"Clever Lily," said Lottie. "That's where you've been hiding. You've built a new home for yourself."

She was no longer afraid of the spider, and became fascinated with watching what Lily got up to. Flies, moths and lots of other tiny flying insects became trapped in the web. When Lily detected something in her web, she came out of the funnel, retrieved the prey, and took it back into the funnel to eat. After a while the web became larger, and Lily was joined by another spider who looked just like her, but he was bigger and his body was darker.

Lottie relayed this news to her mother. "Mum, Lily has a mate," she announced cheerfully.

The two spiders lived in the web happily for a few more weeks until one day there appeared hundreds of tiny eggs. Not long afterwards, Lily was alone again, and the tiny eggs began to hatch, producing lots of tiny baby spiderlings. Lottie briefly wondered where the other spider had gone, but was glad to see that Lily Longlegs had finally found a place safe enough for her baby spiders.

"I'm so glad you came back all those times," said Lottie. "It's been really interesting."

4   TALKING ABOUT THE STORY

- Why was Lottie afraid of the spider?
- What creatures are you afraid of, and why?
- What type of spider do you think Lily Longlegs is?
- Why do you think Lily was alone again at the end of the story?
- What do spiders eat?
- What are spiders' homes made from, and how are they constructed?
- Why do some people think spiders are a good thing to have in the home? (For example, to keep fly numbers down.)

Points for discussion

- Fear of spiders is very common. Discuss this with the children. Are they afraid of spiders or other insects such as wasps. Why are they afraid? Discuss the concept of fear and uncertainty and how this can lead to other emotions and feelings that might be harmful. For example, leading to prejudice and intolerance. Spiders move very quickly, and in some countries spiders can be poisonous so there is reason to fear a bite from a spider. In the UK, spiders are not poisonous, and perform a useful function in the home as they help to keep flies and other insects under control. Fear is often an irrational response and something that is transferred among people. Uncertainty and a lack of knowledge and information can fuel fear, but in the case of spiders and other insects, this can easily be allayed through knowledge and information.
- Spiders are predators. Children can learn about predator/prey relationships and food webs by closely observing how insects and other small creatures function in and around their homes and gardens. Discuss these topics with the children, encouraging them to investigate and explore the micro habitats in their own houses.
- Spiders are part of an ecosystem. Biodiversity is an important part of an ecosystem, with each species performing an important function. We often think of ecosystems being large areas such as forests or marine environments, but there are many examples of micro ecosystems in our homes and gardens. Discuss the importance of biodiversity in these microsystems with the children and how the different species of flora and fauna interrelate and interact with each other.

5   LEARNING ACTIVITIES

Appreciation

We build our homes in a variety of different places, and so do other creatures. A variety of smaller creatures share our homes with us. Some live with us all year round, while others visit us from time to time. Some creatures, such as swallows in the summer, travel thousands of miles to stay with us.

Think of the many different creatures that share our homes. Children live in different types of homes. Make a list of the different types of homes that humans live in, and compare and contrast this with a list of homes that smaller creatures live in who share our living spaces. Birds' nests and spiders' webs are beautifully constructed and perfectly designed for their purpose. Discuss this with the children, and the different types of materials other creatures use.

Some of the creatures we share our living spaces with are commonplace and it is easy to ignore them. Encourage the children to look at creatures in their own home more closely. Moths and spiders have beautiful patterns on their wings. Some spiders have bright colours on their bodies, and birds have brightly coloured wings. The children can do a painting of a creature of their choice, or they can try to recreate the home of a creature through sculpture. Next the children should write a description of the creature and its home, and the dangers it faces on a daily basis. What does the creature eat? Is the creature eaten by other creatures in the home? What materials does it use to build its home? Finally, the children can use their description as the setting for a story of their own.

Building homes – design and technology

Ask the children to choose the home of a creature in their home or garden, such as a spider, a bird, bees and wasps, ants. Provide a range of materials for the children to work with to construct a model of the creature's home. The children can work in small groups or they could work as a whole class to produce a larger model.

List of materials

- Paper and card
- Clay
- Drinking straws
- Sticks and twigs
- Feathers
- Wool and cotton

After the children have completed their models, spend time holding a class discussion about the properties of the structure they have tried to recreate.

- How strong is the structure?
- What are its functions? i.e. to provide shelter, to protect the young from predators, etc.
- What materials did their chosen creature use to construct their home?
- What are the properties of the structure?

Creepy crawlies

The children can carry out an experiment to see how many creepy crawlies they can find. It is easy to attract small insects and invertebrates by cutting a grapefruit in half, and scooping out the flesh. Place the two halves, hollow surface down, outside in a sheltered area on a patch of soil or bare ground. Leave them out overnight. The next morning, the children can investigate the different creatures that have been attracted to the grapefruit. Try to identify the different species, and discuss with the children the various functions the creatures perform. Older children can carry out more detailed research using the bulk library loan or IT suite.

Note: remind the children to return the small creatures to where they found them, and be careful not to harm them.

Conservation

We think of conservation as an activity that takes place in countries far away involving exotic creatures such as tigers, whales and dolphins, gorillas, and so on. Which creatures that share our homes need conserving? Some bird and bat species are endangered, for example.

Conservation activities in a home or school setting often involve providing habitats for creatures to live in. It can also involve not doing damage or harm to some creatures in our home environment that we consider to be a nuisance such as wasps and bees or spiders and ants. Some creatures are protected by law such as certain species of bats and owls, and it is illegal to kill them or remove them from your home without specialist help.

As a class project, build an ant farm or formicarium. See page 13 for instructions.

Protection and enhancement

How can we protect the creatures in our homes? What about creatures that become a nuisance to us such as mice, flies, ants and other insects? How can we discourage creatures coming into our homes that we don't want there without harming or destroying them?

Some bird species in the UK have been declining rapidly in the past two to three decades. The house sparrow was once very common, but its numbers are now drastically reduced.

The Royal Society for the Protection of Birds (RSPB) has a lot of useful information for children about the different types of birds that either live in the UK or that visit from different countries. Some of these build nests in the eaves of our houses and share our living space.

Arrange for an RSPB member of staff to visit the school. Or contact your local RSPB and get the class involved in bird survey work as a project.

Picture activity

Give each child a photocopy of the picture provided. Use this as a springboard into creative writing – a poem, a description or story. And/or for a research project, using the school library, the bulk library loan and IT suite, how much can the children find out about spiders and/or daffodils?

Additional learning activities

*   Create model insects or birds using recycled materials such as egg boxes, plastic bottles, drinking straws, etc.
*   Create insect or butterfly mobiles for the classroom.
*   Using a map of the world, chart migration routes of different bird species.

Continued . . .

WILD CREATURES THAT SHARE OUR HOMES

Below are just a few of the wild creatures that share our homes with us. Can you think of any more?

Birds

Blackbird
House sparrow
House martin
Swift

Mammals

Bats
Mice
Squirrel

Insects

Ants
Bees
Beetles
Bluebottle
Butterfly
Housefly
Moths
Silverfish
Spider
Wasps
Woodlice

Amphibians

Frogs
Toads

MINIBEAST ZOOKEEPER – BUILDING AN ANT FARM OR FORMICARIUM

Building an ant farm is relatively easy, and provides children with first-hand experience of the life of insects.

Equipment and materials

A large jar or small aquarium with a tight lid
Small bottle
Small garden shovel
Bucket
Garden soil
Ants

Funnel
Strong paper or fabric
Scotch tape
Honey or sugar water
Cotton ball
Water

You will need to construct the farm in such a way that the ants can be viewed through the glass. This can be achieved by placing a small glass container inside a larger one or by using a small aquarium. The smaller container takes up space in the middle of the main container so the ants build along the glass so you can view them.

You will need to find an ant colony in the school grounds or in the local park. You can also purchase ants for ant farms by post (check your local directories or the internet for suppliers). Ideally, you will need a queen ant (with wings). When you have found a colony, dig in an area where you see a lot of ants and put some of this soil with ants inside, into a bucket. Try to get the queen ant into your bucket if possible, along with eggs and larvae.

Using a funnel or paper cone, place soil into the main container away from the smaller container. Fill the space between the containers with this soil. The smaller container can be filled with ordinary garden soil. Ants can climb most materials, even glass, so make sure you put a lid on the container. The ants will need to breathe so ensure you have some air holes, but take care that they are not too large or the ants will be able to escape.

Ants usually live underground so the ant farm will need to be in darkness for much of the time. Cover the container with thick paper or fabric. Ants love sweet foods. You can feed your ants with a drop of honey or bread dripped in sugar water in their container. You can also add small bits of fruit or vegetables. Make sure you give the ants some water by soaking a cotton ball and placing this in the container every few days.

Record the ants' activities by keeping a log or diary. Observe the life-cycle of the ants from egg to larvae to adult ant. Observe how they construct their home, how they interact with each other, and which ants do different types of work.

Older children can research more about ants and other insects using the IT suite.

PICTURE ACTIVITY

PICTURE ACTIVITY

My Home is an Ecosystem

Theme: Understanding and protecting creatures that share our homes

Introduction

The assembly leader introduces the theme and talks about the diversity of creatures that share our homes with us.

Give examples of this such as the birds that fly thousands of miles to spend summer in this country and which build their nests under the eaves of our houses. Or beneficial creatures such as spiders which help to control flies and other insects.

Story

The assembly leader reminds the children that there are many different creatures that share our homes. Sometimes we are afraid of the creatures because they may sting us or they run quickly and frighten us. The assembly leader or a child reads the story about Lottie and Lily Longlegs.

Alternatively, the children could read one or more of their own spider stories, and/or some of the information they researched about the creatures that share our home.

Song

Select a song which is relevant to the theme or which echoes the story in some way.

Examples

I Love God's Tiny Creatures
In *Someone's Singing, Lord* (A&C Black)

Little Birds in Winter Time
In *Someone's Singing, Lord* (A&C Black)

Poem

Select a suitable poem. Alternatively, you can have a child (or children) read the poems they chose in class. Additionally, some of the children could read their descriptions of their favourite creatures which share their homes.

Quiet reflection or prayer

For a universal, humanistic or multi-faith assembly:

The assembly leader says:
Think of all the creatures that share our homes and living spaces with us, from the beautiful swallows that fly here in the summer, moths with beautiful wings, and spiders that help to keep our homes free from flies (pause). Think about the smaller creatures around us and how we can help them to live their lives free from harm (pause). Think about the variety of creatures and the functions they perform (pause).

Or for Christian schools:

Let us pray.

Dear Lord

Help us to live alongside the many creatures that share our homes with us and to understand them. Teach us to appreciate that life is precious and even the creatures we are afraid of deserve our respect.

Amen.

CHAPTER 2

My Garden

Theme Two: My Garden

This chapter explores the wonder of the natural world in our garden and the creatures who share our living spaces, and how they survive.

Gardens are fascinating places. They provide us with food and recreation, and an outdoor living space. Gardens come in a variety of shapes and sizes from window boxes to larger formal gardens with trees and a wide variety of plants and flowers.

Environmental Values

- Appreciation: Appreciation of the flora and fauna in the garden.
- Conservation: Conserving creatures and habitats in the garden.
- Protection and enhancement: Valuing biodiversity in the garden.

A Suggested Lesson Plan

1 Introduce the theme

How can we learn to understand and appreciate nature in our garden? The garden is a good place to start learning more about food cycles and food chains, gaining an understanding of where our own food comes from and how other animals obtain their food. It is also a good environment for starting to learn about biodiversity. Even the smallest of gardens can be home to a wide variety of different species.

2 Vocabulary

The teacher ensures that the children understand the words given.

3 The story

The teacher shows the illustration and reads the story.

4 **Talking about the story**

The teacher uses some of the questions and discussion points given, stimulating the children to talk about the story/theme.

5 **Learning activities**

The story activities encourage listening and discussion skills. Follow-up activities introduce the concepts of biodiversity, ecosystems, food webs, and the relationships between different creatures and plantlife.

1 INTRODUCE THE THEME

* Which creatures share our gardens?
* What do they eat? Are they plant eating animals or carnivores?
* What do other creatures live in and how do they build their homes?
* What can we grow in our gardens that we can eat for food?
* What can we do to provide a better habitat for wild creatures in our gardens? For example, encouraging bees and butterflies, and different birds.

2 VOCABULARY

Story vocabulary

Hive	–	*home for bees*
Nectar	–	*sweet, sticky substance in flowers used to attract pollinating birds and insects*
Pollen	–	*tiny yellow grains in flowers which are transferred to other similar flowers as part of the plant reproduction process*
Alighted	–	*landed on*
Bellows	–	*a device with an air bag that pushes out air when squeezed*
Hexagonal	–	*a six-sided shape*
Populations	–	*inhabitants of a place or country*

Associated environmental vocabulary

Pollination	–	*the process of transferring pollen between flowers of a similar kind for the reproduction of plants*
Decomposers	–	*small insects and bacteria that break down dead matter*
Invertebrates	–	*creatures without a backbone*
Larvae	–	*part of the life-cycle of certain species of insects*

No Honey for Breakfast

Sara loved honey for breakfast. Each morning she would spread a thick layer on her toast with some slices of banana. Sometimes her Mummy would make delicious pancakes, and that was even better than toast for spreading honey. This morning Sara was very concerned. She had heard on the radio that all the bees were dying and very soon there would be no more honey. Sara couldn't imagine having no honey for breakfast. You could keep your jams and peanut butter; honey was a food fit for queens and princesses. The bees themselves had a queen who gave birth to the baby bees, and made sure that the thousands of worker bees kept the hive in order.

Sara studied the jar of honey thoughtfully. Already it was half empty. What if her Mummy could not buy any more honey? What would she do for breakfast? Why were the bees dying? What was making them so sick? When Sara was sick, her mother tucked her up in bed, read her stories and gave her lots of milky drinks, sweetened with honey, of course. Perhaps Sara could help to make the bees better, and then she would still be able to have honey for breakfast. But what could she do? Sara didn't know anything about bees so she decided to find out.

Outside in the garden, Sara sat and watched as a little bee alighted onto a beautiful lilac-coloured buddleia bush. For a few minutes Sara watched fascinated as the bee flew from flower to flower drinking the nectar and gathering pollen. It was a very busy little bee, and soon its legs were heavy and swollen with yellow dust. For almost an hour, Sara watched as lots of other bees visited the bush, each flying away with its little cargo of sweet nectar and pollen. Some larger bees also visited. They seemed a lot heavier than the tiny bees and bumbled from flower to flower, taking longer than the little bees, which darted here and there.

The very next day, Sara asked her Mummy if she would take her to Cloudberry Farm. She knew the farmer there had bees because they sometimes bought honey from the Farm Shop, and this was the same honey that was sold in the local shop.

Later that day at Cloudberry Farm, Mr Gray, the farmer, was just about to collect some honey and said that Sara could help him, but first she would have to put on a special suit to protect her face and arms, just in case the bees got frightened and tried to sting her. Sara had to wear a hat with netting all around it that covered her face and neck. Then she put on special gloves and a cream coloured smock. Mr Gray did the same.

The hive was busy, and Sara was relieved to see so many bees going in and out of the slots. She wondered whether these were the same bees that visited her buddleia bush in the garden.

Mr Gray had a small can with a funny looking nozzle on the end and which had bellows on the side. He used this to blow some smoke into the entrance of the hive. Suddenly all the bees flew out and away. Some settled on the mesh net covering Sara's face and she could hear them buzzing angrily at being disturbed. But they too flew away after a while.

Mr Gray removed a frame from the hive and Sara could see that it was filled with a beautiful pattern of hexagonal shapes, all filled with a golden liquid. Mr Gray used a special cutter to remove a section of the comb and then placed it into a container.

"Mr Gray, is it true that bees are dying?" asked Sara.

"Sadly, it is true, Sara," he replied. "It's awful what is happening to the bees, and no-one really knows what is causing so many of them to die. Some people are blaming the mobile phone masts for confusing the bees with their radio signals. Others say the bees have diseases, but it's hard to find the real cause."

He went on to explain to Sara how important bees are by helping all the plants to pollinate so that they can produce their fruits and seeds. "Without bees," he said, "we are all in real trouble. We won't be able to produce crops, or vegetables and the fruit trees will have no fruit."

"What can we do to help the bees get better?" asked Sara, who was very upset by this news.

"There isn't much anyone can do right now. We can only wait and hope that the bees get stronger."

"But your bees are OK, aren't they?" she asked.

"For now," said Mr Gray with a serious look.

"Then we must look after your bees, and make sure they don't get sick," Sara said, in a determined voice.

Mr Gray smiled. "I could do with a helper," he said. "There's a lot of work involved in keeping bees."

All through the summer holidays, Sara helped Mr Gray with his bees. Every week there were reports in the news about the decline in bee populations. These were very worrying, but Sara tried to stay positive. At least their bees were doing well, and for now that's all Sara could think about. It gave her some comfort to be involved in keeping bees, and Sara had learned such a lot about them. She knew she couldn't stop all the bees from dying, but she could help Mr Gray with his bees, and they would continue to make lots of honey for her breakfast.

4 TALKING ABOUT THE STORY

- Why are bees important for plants and flowers?
- Where do bees live?
- How do bees interact with each other in family groups?
- Why do you think bees are dying?
- What does Sara have to wear to protect herself from being stung?
- How does Mr Gray get the honey from the bee hive?

Points for discussion

- Bees are pollinators and a key component in the ecosystem for plant reproduction. Without bees many of our crops, vegetable plants, flowers and trees would not produce flowers and fruits.
- The buddleia bush is sometimes called the butterfly bush because it attracts various species of butterflies. Discuss this with the children, and the different plants and shrubs that we can put in our gardens to attract wildlife.
- There are lots of insects that share our gardens. Some of these are beneficial and some are pests. Discuss the different types of insects and their functions in the garden. What about creatures that live in the soil, such as worms?

5 LEARNING ACTIVITIES

Appreciation

Gardens are a place to relax outside the home as well as providing us with food. They are also home to many different creatures.

Wildlife and kitchen gardening

Create a garden that attracts a variety of wildlife. This can be a small garden project using a range of tubs and containers filled with different flowers and plants that attract butterflies, bees and other insects. Or it can be a larger conservation project if there is sufficient suitable space in the school grounds. In this activity, older children can design and plan the wildlife garden, and research the different types of plants. Younger children can help to design and plan a garden through colourful drawings and paintings, choosing flowers with their teacher's assistance that will attract bees and butterflies.

For a longer term project, the children could grow some vegetables and herbs and learn about the nutritional benefits of fresh, homegrown foods. The children could learn to make simple dishes from the vegetables.

Older children could learn about food miles and food processing, researching the environmental impact of foods that are shipped around the globe.

Through growing plants and vegetables for food, children will learn about life cycles.

Conservation

We often think of conservation as an activity that takes place in countries far away involving exotic creatures such as tigers, whales and dolphins, gorillas, and so on. Which creatures that share our homes need conserving? Some bird and bat species are endangered, for example.

Research local conservation organisations such as Wildlife Trusts, RSPB, the Butterfly Conservation Organisation. You can arrange a visit from these organisations or encourage the children to get involved in conservation projects for particular species of plants or animals.

Some organisations have reserves that the children can visit to learn about different aspects of the garden.

Protection and enhancement

How can we protect the creatures in our homes? What about creatures that become a nuisance to us such as mice, flies and other insects?

Protecting habitats is an important part of wildlife conservation. Even the smallest of gardens can provide good habitats for insects, birds and small mammals. Conservation or wildlife areas are ideal for a wide range of cross-curricular learning activities for children from planting seeds and plants to grow flowers and vegetables to carrying out basic survey work on plants and animals.

The children can learn about the plants that are most beneficial for certain species, and which insects, birds and other species are beneficial to plants.

Learning about the life cycles of a variety of plants and animals is also fascinating for children. In Chapter 8, there is an activity for children on the Butterfly Lifecycle. This could be replicated for other species, for example frogs and toads have a dramatic metamorphosis.

The opportunities for learning in the "outdoor classroom" are many, and require only minimal instruction or guidance for the children. Exploring the natural world for themselves stimulates the children's curiosity and imagination.

- **Beneficial Relationships** – Explore the symbiotic relationships of different plant and animal species. How does this co-operation work, and what are the benefits to both species? What if one of the species was no longer there, what would happen to the other? The garden has many examples of symbiotic relationships such as bees pollinating flowers, ladybirds protecting plants from aphids, frogs and toads keeping slugs and snails under control.

- **Insect or Bug Hunt** – With some very basic equipment and materials, the children can conduct a bug hunt or survey. Visit at least three different areas such as playground, field, woodland, in hedgerows and around buildings (under ledges, doorsteps, etc). Record where the insects were found and what type of habitat. What are the insect's special characteristics. What stage of the life cycle is the insect at? Use the internet or a field study guide to identify different species. Encourage the children to look under rotting logs or wood, and under rocks and stones. Remind them not to disturb or harm the insects, and to replace any insects they move back to where they found them. Back in the classroom discuss some of the functions that insects carry out that are good for the garden such as decomposing dead matter, keeping pests under control, and so on.

Picture activity

Give each child a photocopy of the picture provided. Use this as a springboard into creative writing – a poem, a description or story. And/or for a research project, using the school library, the bulk library loan and IT suite, how much can the children find out about robins and/or the buddleia bushes?

Additional learning activities

- Make a cast of animal footprints following the instructions on the photocopiable page.
- Explore how plants drink water by splitting the stem of a pale flower with a long stem and placing one half of the stem in a clear glass of water, and the other in a glass containing red food dye. The flower will stay pale on one side, and will be tinged with red on the side with the food dye. As the water evaporates into the air, it leaves the dye behind in the petals. Discuss plant structures with the children and how there are separate mini tubes within the stem that take the water to the flower.
- Study a range of flowers by collecting a selection, complete with their leaves and stems. Remind the children to be careful when picking wild flowers. Press the flowers into a book and place under a heavy weight such as further books, or if you have a flower press you can use this. Leave the flowers for two weeks. Carefully remove the weights and arrange the dried flowers on a class collage or in a nature diary. Try to identify the flowers and plants, and discuss the functions of the various parts of the plant. Explore the different uses we have for various plants: food, medicine, fuel, etc.

Continued . . .

THINGS SARA FOUND OUT ABOUT BEES

Fascinating facts about bees

- There are approximately 260 species of bees in the UK.
- Honey bees have highly organised social structures. Up to half a million can live in a hive at any one time.
- The hive of a honey bee is made up of hexagonal structures which form the comb where honey is stored. This shape is the most efficient for storing honey.
- Each hive has a queen bee and drones and worker bees. The drones are male bees and it is their job to mate with the queen to produce larvae. The workers are female. It is their job to bring nectar back to the hive.
- The earliest records of beekeeping are in 7000 BC in cave paintings in Spain.
- In 4000 BC, Egyptians started to use honey to sweeten food and also as an embalming agent.
- Until the Second World War, honey was widely used for its antibacterial qualities in dressing wounds.
- Today, nearly one million tonnes of honey is produced worldwide every year.
- Bees pollinate a large number of our crops, and are vital for plant reproduction.

What other interesting facts can you find about bees?

★

★

★

★

★

MAKE A CAST OF ANIMAL TRACKS

Materials

- Strip of thin card, or cut a strip from a discarded 2 litre bottle. The card or plastic needs to be 25 cm (10 in) long and 4 cm (1.5 in) wide.
- Paperclips
- Jug or bottle of water
- Mixing bowl or bucket
- Plaster of Paris
- Spoon
- Water (for cleaning the cast)
- Old toothbrush or small soft scrubbing brush
- Toothpicks

Instructions

1. Find some animal tracks in muddy or sandy areas of the school grounds, or in the local park. Try to find tracks that are in moist, firm mud. When you have found some tracks, look for the clearest ones that show as many features of the animal's foot as possible.
2. Clear the area of any debris such as twigs, leaves and small stones. Be careful not to disturb the tracks. Place the strip of cardboard or plastic carefully around the tracks, forming a ring. Secure with paperclips and then push the ring firmly into the ground around the tracks.
3. Mix some plaster of Paris into the bowl or bucket with water from your jug or bottle. Stir the mixture continually with the spoon until you have a slightly runny paste.
4. Pour the mixed plaster into the ring, and smooth the top.
5. Leave the plaster to set for at least 15 minutes.
6. Carefully lift the plaster and the ring and take it back to school or home and leave for a further 24 hours to set completely.
7. Brush off the mud or sand with a brush. You can use a toothpick to pick the mud out of fiddly areas such as claw prints.
8. Try to identify which animal made the print.
9. If the cast is a good one, you can make more casts from this by making a print in a deep tray filled with sand, and by repeating the process above.

POLLINATION

Information sheet

Flowering plants and flowers need pollination to be able to reproduce. Once a flower has been pollinated it produces seeds, which are then dispersed by animals or by the wind, and a new plant can then grow from the seed.

Flowers are made up of different male and female parts:

Petal	petals can be brightly coloured or patterned to attract bees, butterflies, birds and insects
Sepal	a special type of leaves that form a ring round the petals to protect the flower when it is still a bud. All the sepals together are called a "calyx"
Stamen	the stamen has two parts: the anther and filament. The anther produces the pollen and the filament holds the anther, allowing it to move
Stigma	the stigma is sticky and collects the pollen
Style	the style holds the stigma in place
Pistil	the pistil contains the female parts of the flower
Ovary	the ovary contains the ovules

Wind pollination

Some flowers have pollen that is light enough to be carried by the wind to other plants.

Helping with pollination

Some flowers need help with pollination and attract insects and birds using scent, colour or nectar, which is a sweet sticky substance. Some flowers have honey-guides on their petals such as spots, dots or lines which act as a signpost, directing the insects to the nectar. As the nectar is gathered, pollen grains attach themselves to the legs and hairs of the creatures, and as they go from flower to flower, the pollen grains are distributed.

PICTURE ACTIVITY

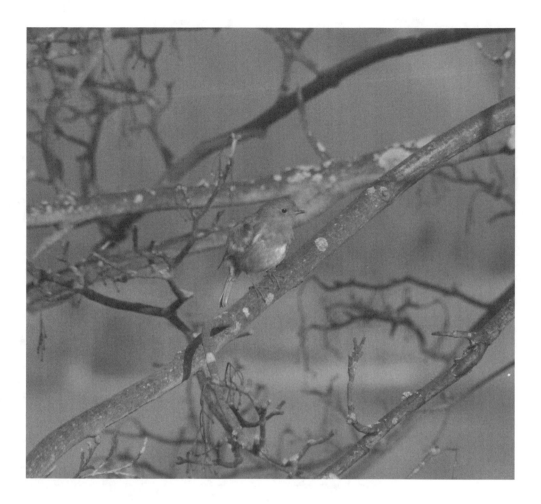

PICTURE ACTIVITY

My Garden

Theme: Protecting and enjoying the garden environment

Introduction

The assembly leader introduces the theme and talks about the importance of gardens, how they provide us with food, a place to relax and a variety of habitats for a diverse range of creatures.

Story

The assembly leader reminds the children that gardens can be ideal habitats for lots of different creatures and we can help them by planting trees, plants and flowers that provide food. Bees rely on flowers for nectar and pollen, and help our crops to grow.

  The assembly leader or one of the children can read the story: *No Honey for Breakfast.*

  Alternatively, the children could read one or more of their own nature stories, or some of the information they researched about the birds, butterflies, bees and other insects and small mammals that share our gardens.

Song

Select a song which is relevant to the theme or which echoes the story in some way.

Examples

Buzz a Buzz a Bumble Bee
In *Jump into the Ring* (Ward Lock Educational)

Tiny Creatures
In *Sing as you Grow* (Ward Lock Educational)

Think of a world without any flowers
In *Someone's Singing Lord* (A&C Black)

Song of Life
In *Every Colour Under the Sun* (Ward Lock Educational)

Poem

Select a suitable poem. Alternatively, you can have a child (or children) read the poems they chose in class. Additionally, some of the children could read their descriptions of their favourite creatures which share their homes.

Here is the Beehive
In *This Little Puffin* (Young Puffin)

In the Garden in Winter
In *The Squirrel in Town* (Blackie)

Quiet reflection or prayer

For a universal, humanistic or multi-faith assembly:

The assembly leader says:
Let us think of our gardens as beautiful places that provide us with food, a place to relax, and a habitat for lots of different creatures (pause). Let us think about the many ways we can help the birds, bees, butterflies and insects in our gardens by building shelters, and growing plants and flowers that provide them with food.

Or for Christian schools:

Let us pray.

God the creator,

Thank you for all our beautiful gardens, and for the food we grow there, and for the creatures who live among the plants, trees and flowers and help our garden to grow. Help us to think about how we can help the plants and animals in our gardens.

Amen.

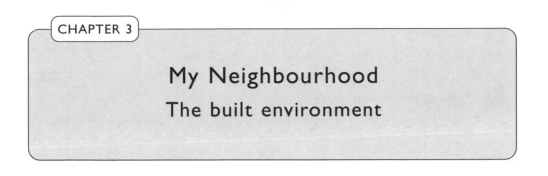

CHAPTER 3

My Neighbourhood
The built environment

Theme Three: My Neighbourhood: the built environment

Many children live in towns and cities and can learn to appreciate the buildings and the amenities as well as the green spaces of their area, and understand how to conserve, protect and enhance the built environment. It is important that children understand about the variety of flora and fauna which share the built environment, and which have adapted to live alongside humans. Children who live in rural areas will visit or eventually work in urban environments and should have some appreciation of the issues.

Environmental Values

*   Appreciation: To appreciate urban facilities and the flora and fauna which share the built environment.
*   Conservation: To reduce pollution including excessive packaging, to buy locally-grown produce, and to learn to co-exist with diverse species in the built environment.
*   Protection and enhancement: to reduce litter and dirt and enhance the urban environment with plants, trees etc.

A Suggested Lesson Plan

1 Introduce the theme

We need to look after our towns and cities through promoting cleaner air and water for human health, by reducing grime and litter and by improving the visual environment, with, for example, less graffiti and more plants and trees.

2 Vocabulary

The teacher ensures that the children understand the words given.

3 The story

The teacher shows the illustration and reads the story.

4 Talking about the story

The teacher uses some of the questions and discussion points given, stimulating the children to talk about the story/theme.

5 Learning activities

The story and associated activities encourage listening and discussion skills. Follow-up activities introduce environmental appreciation and understanding in the context of the built environment.

1 INTRODUCE THE THEME

- When we shop we need to reduce the amount of the packaging on the goods we buy and where possible recycle "rubbish". We could reduce traffic pollution by buying local produce or by growing some of our own fruit and vegetables.
- We could also reduce traffic pollution by using public transport and car sharing.
- We must play our part in reducing dirt, graffiti and litter.
- We should enhance the visual environment, for example, by creating beautiful gardens and parks.

2 VOCABULARY

Story vocabulary

Chucked	–	*threw*
Container	–	*something to hold things in*
Crouching	–	*bending low*
Fertiliser	–	*enriching substance for soil*
Admired	–	*looked up to*
Design	–	*make a pattern*
Dumped	–	*threw down or threw away*
Mess	–	*untidy muddle*
Litter	–	*untidy and discarded refuse or rubbish*
Litter lout	–	*someone who leaves litter*
Septic	–	*infected cut or wound*
Tilted	–	*tipped to one side*

Associated environmental vocabulary

Amenities	—	*facilities*
Urban creatures	—	*animals living in towns and cities*
Air pollution	—	*contamination of the air, for example, by smoke*
Recycling	—	*reusing discarded materials*
Packaging	—	*the wrapping for food and other goods*
Local produce	—	*food (example, fruit and vegetables) which is grown in the areas nearby*
Public transport	—	*buses, trains, trams*

Continued . . .

Litter Lessons

© Mal Leicester, Denise Taylor, Taryn Shrigley-Wightman, Routledge 2009

Litter Lessons

"Pick that up, Jack," Mum called. "This minute."

"Sorry," I said.

I was watering my patch of the garden and had chucked an empty plant-food container into the hedge. I picked it up and went to the bin by our gate. Shandy, my new sheepdog puppy, trotted after me. She's dead cute. She began to circle me, crouching every now and then as though I were a herd of sheep.

On the way back to the house I stopped for a final look at my plot. It was looking great. I'd been allowed to plant what I wanted so long as I looked after it. I'd dug into the bare ground, uncovering rich, dark soil beneath the hard crust. I'd chucked out stones and dug in fertiliser and grown thick, low flowers which completely covered the large square of bare soil in a pattern of green leaves and bright colours, framed by white blossom all round the edge.

"Hard work and imagination," Dad had said.

Shandy stood by my side and we admired it together. Everyone liked my design. It had been worth the hard work.

Back in the house Mum immediately asked me to go out to the bin again, with a black plastic bag of kitchen rubbish.

At the door I found my friend Tom, on his bike. He had been just about to knock.

"Coming for a ride?" he asked.

"Yeah sure," I said. "I'll take this later." I dumped the black bag by the door, popped Shandy safely back inside the house and collected my bike from the shed. We had a great time, me and Tom, riding through the fields. We came across some dumped beer bottles and scored points for hitting them with a stone from quite a long way. It came out a draw. On the way home we rode down Bude Hill, no hands.

Luckily we reached home just before it poured with rain. Shandy came running to meet me, her tail wagging furiously. She was always dead pleased to see me. I bent down, pushing her about in a play-fight which she loved.

At bedtime Shandy followed me up the stairs and when I settled down in bed with my Harry Potter book, she curled up beside me. It was cosy until Mum came up to switch off the light.

"Just look at this mess," she said, frowning at my room. My clothes and things littered the floor.

"You can pick all this up tomorrow, Jack. You're turning into a real litter lout. And Shandy can't sleep there either." She kissed me good-night and carried Shandy downstairs.

I listened to the rain rattling hard on my window. I liked the drumming sound and when I drifted off to sleep I dreamed that I was drumming on a big black, plastic drum and the clothes on my bedroom floor rose into the air and, like big cloth birds, they flapped round the room before flying out of the window.

The dream was so vivid that I was almost surprised to find my clothes were still there in the morning, though when I began to get dressed, I discovered that my T-shirt was missing. It was my favourite. My Man United. Could it really have blown out of the window? I parted the curtains and looked out. I had a shock. The garden was littered with rubbish: soggy newspaper, packages, tins and cartons were strewn everywhere, including on my patch too. I pulled on an ordinary T-shirt and ran downstairs to the garden. I saw immediately that Shandy had chewed a hole in the black bag which I'd left by the door. She'd scattered the rubbish everywhere. She'd trampled some of the plants in my flower design, playing with the rubbish.

"You bad pup," I said crossly, dismayed by my ruined garden. She hung her head.

"Don't blame Shandy," Mum called from the door. "You left the bag, and you can pick it all up before breakfast."

Shandy stayed with me and licked my hand as I collected up the rubbish. I was still cross with her and pushed her away.

After it was done I was ravenous, but as I bolted down my cornflakes I noticed something screwed up in a corner near Shandy's bed. I picked it up. It was my lost T-shirt, well chewed and even more spoiled than my garden.

"Oh Shandy!" I said, sadly.

She gave a small, uncertain shake of her tail.

"Puppies chew," said Mum. "You mustn't leave your clothes on the floor."

There and then I was made to go and tidy my room. What a rotten day it was turning out to be. It got even worse. When we took Shandy up the field for her walk she yelped as she was running and then limped over to us. Mum picked her up, turning over her paw. A piece of glass was stuck there. She was bleeding badly.

"Some idiot has left a broken bottle," Mum said.

I didn't dare confess that it may have been me.

In the vet's waiting room, poor Shandy was shaking with fear. I stroked her, telling her softly that it would be soon be better. I was sorry I'd been mad at her and so sorry that I had left that broken glass. I hated having to hold her while the vet pulled it out.

"She'll be OK as long as it doesn't go septic," he said.

Every night that week, as gently as I could, I bathed Shandy's paw. She watched, her head tilted to one side. She knew I was trying to help. After a few days, she was running about again – back to her same old self. I had changed though. I had learned a lesson that I would never forget.

Acknowledgement: This story was previously published in *Stories for Circle Time and Assembly* (2006) by Mal Leicester, published by Routledge.

The Story

4 TALKING ABOUT THE STORY

- What four things did Jack do to create his garden?
- Why was Jack's room a mess?
- How had Jack's garden become littered with rubbish?
- Why might the glass that cut Shandy have been left there by Jack?
- What lesson had Jack learnt in the end?

Points for discussion

- The litter from the black plastic bag had spoilt Jack's garden. Discuss refuse and recycling with the children. Does their family rubbish have to be separated into different bins? Why is that? (Recycling)
- How can we reduce the amount of rubbish we produce? (recycling; less packaging)
- Discuss the dangers of litter (cutting children and creatures; flapping onto car windscreens; plastic bags can suffocate young children and creatures)
- Discuss other pollutants (dirt, grime, exhaust fumes, noise pollution, graffiti and vandalism). (Note: not all graffiti is bad. Some graffiti enhances urban environments through artistic expression.)
- Discuss ways in which we can improve our built environment – making it less dangerous and more enjoyable, more pleasant to look at and spend our leisure time in.

5 LEARNING ACTIVITIES

Appreciation

Urban nature walk

1. Create a nature trail
   Take the children on a walk through the school grounds and out into the neighbourhood. If possible take a walk that passes local gardens and can pass through a local park. The children note plants, wild flowers, beautiful trees and notable buildings/statues, etc. Back in class they draw a map (with written instructions beneath) so that other children can follow the nature trail they have created. The first group will enjoy spotting the natural objects that they use to create their nature trail and subsequent children will enjoy finding these.
2. Record city noises
   On a similar walk the children can record the noises they hear – bird song, traffic, car horns, dogs barking, alarms, leaves rustling and wind in trees, sounds of water, people calling, children laughing and playing, etc. Back in the classroom play some of the recordings as a way into a discussion about noise pollution and the value of silence. Which noises were pleasant and which were unpleasant?

Conservation

Recycle your rubbish

The aim of this session is to show the children how it is possible to recycle using used materials that are otherwise regarded as rubbish. Encourage the children to bring in boxes, cardboard rolls, old plastic bottles with lids, fabric, ribbon, string, etc that would otherwise be discarded as litter at home that week. Perhaps they can also bring in discarded Christmas, birthday and postcards and broken games or toys and old hats that are going to be thrown away. The children will enjoy turning this junk into gifts for themselves and their families and for classroom displays.

Ensure that the seeds of the idea of recycling have been sown! Begin by explaining that recycling helps to conserve our planet's resources.

Hold up some of the objects that children have brought in and have a class brainstorm session:

"What could we use this for?"
"What could we make out of this?"

You will provide glue, paint, scissors. Give the children the photocopiable pages. They can select a gift to make either for themselves or for a grown up family member or for a younger brother or sister/baby. If there is time and they have brought in sufficient "litter" they could make more than one gift. They do not need to be restricted to the suggestions, but could use an idea of their own.

Protection and enhancement

Environment litter hunt/poster

Who can collect the most litter? Have a session where the children are allowed out into the playground and playing fields to collect any litter they can find.

Once back in the classroom, the children can draw a map showing where litter was found. Older children could repeat the exercise for the whole neighbourhood, i.e. collect litter, map the local neighbourhood, mark the places where litter was found.

Discuss with the children how the litter has come to be discarded. Who is responsible for dropping the litter and why?

Alternatively, they can make a class environment chart. First show the children a "forbid" sign, for example, a No Smoking sign. Such signs are in a red circle with a red line "crossing out" the forbidden activity. Give each child a card and they can each make a picture forbidding **one** of the pollutants. For example, no litter or no noise pollution or no graffiti. These pictures can be used as a border for the class environment chart.

Finally, brainstorm with the children simple rules that will help to make the classroom a more pleasant environment. Include things like "no litter", but also enhancement suggestions like: let us keep and water green plants, let us make an interesting display and beautiful pictures.

Picture activity

Give each child a photocopy of the picture provided. Use this as a springboard into creative writing: a poem, description or story. And/or for a research project, using the school library, the bulk library loan and IT suite, how much can the children find out about the different activities for children in the built environment and/or nettles?

Additional learning activities

- Living and non-living things

  Have a range of objects on the table in the classroom. Include a plant, a doll, a photograph of a person, and if possible, a creature (example a fish in a bowl). Ask the children to pick out the living from the non-living things. Now ask the children to look out of the classroom window and name some living and non-living things they can see.

  Give each child a copy of the photocopiable page which is a second illustration of the story. Say, "if it was not a picture, what can you pick out that is living (boy, dog, vet) and what is non-living (bandage, scissors, clothes, pens, glasses)?"

  What is a living thing?
  What are the differences between living and non-living things?

  Have a discussion about this. The dictionary defines life as: the state of being alive, conscious existence, plants and animals; and living as: having vitality/life, currently in existence. Non-living things do not have consciousness, are not alive.

- Healthcare speaker

  Invite a speaker, such as a healthcare worker, to visit the children to talk about the importance of looking after our health – including healthy lungs (not smoking; clean air).

- Environmental messages

  Explain to the children that there are values and "messages" in everything we read. What are some of the messages in the story, *Litter Lessons*. Read some poems with fairly obvious values and messages, and see if the children can identify these. Finally, using a library lesson have the children analyse a selection of books to find direct and indirect environmental messages and values. Discuss their findings.

- Selection of relevant poems for the assembly

  Divide the children into small groups and give each group a selection of poetry and song books. Ask them to identify poems and songs that could be used in an environmental assembly. Each group could select one of these poems for one of the group to read to the whole class.

RECYCLING GIFT SUGGESTIONS

For me Treasure box Robot Robot mask Easter bonnet Skittles	**For grown up family member** Jewellery box First aid box Straw fan Book mark Framed picture
For younger brother or sister or baby Animal mobile Framed picture Games box Hand puppets Jigsaw	**For classroom** Junk picture 3-D picture/display board Cardboard sculpture Wall masks Classroom display

GIFT INSTRUCTIONS

Decorative boxes: jewellery, treasure, first aid, games

Encourage the children to select an empty box; small for jewellery; medium for first aid and treasure boxes; and large for games. The boxes should be as sturdy as possible. Minor tears/weaknesses could be strengthened with strong tape. The boxes should be decorated to fit their function. For example:

- Jewellery box – paint in a jewel colour or colours. Line with tissue paper and decorate the lid with glitter, sequins, beads.
- First Aid box – paint and add a red cross using red paint or tape, or glue on red ribbon.
- Treasure box – paint on a treasure island. Use a box with a hinged lid and create some kind of fastener or lock.
- Games box – Cut games illustrations from old magazines and birthday cards to make a games collage on the lid of your box.

Robot

Use boxes to create a robot. With older children they could cut holes for the eyes and cover with red acetate and make a circuit to produce flashing eyes.

Robot mask

Take a piece of medium weight card that will fit around a child's head. Cut out a window for the face. Decorate with buttons and spray with gold or silver paint.

Easter bonnet

This offers scope to be very creative. The children could use an old hat or cap or box and add bright decorations of all kinds.

Fan

The children cut a rounded spade shape (with a small handle) out of cardboard. Tape could be wound around the handle or ribbon glued there. The "spade" part of the fan is then painted decoratively. Straws could be glued in a fan shape over the spade and painted in a contrasting colour.

Framed picture

Choose a picture from an old birthday card. Stick this onto cardboard which is a little bigger than the picture, to provide a frame. Cut out strips of thick cardboard the same size as the frame and paint these before gluing them in place. Choose a colour to complement the picture. Add ribbon or painted string for hanging the picture. Depending on the subject of the picture it could be for your own bedroom or be a gift for a younger child or an adult, or fauna and flora pictures could hang on the classroom wall.

GIFT INSTRUCTIONS

Book mark

Cut out a piece of card about 20cm × 4cm. Give this a pointed end. Stencil or trace the letters of the name of the reader on one side and create a painted design on the other.

Animal mobile

Use a ring of plastic or thick card or a coat hanger as the base. Using string or ribbon hang animal pictures/shapes from this base to create a mobile. Paint the mobile in bright primary colours since it is for a young child's bedroom.

Junk pictures

Take a rectangle of cardboard the size you want for your picture. Paint in the sky and land (or sea). Create your textured pictures by cutting out the shapes from fabrics. To create a 3-D picture paint boxes and junk materials and glue these onto the rectangle.

3-D display

Two sides of a hinged cardboard box could be used to create an L shape (floor and wall) 3-D junk display. Paint a picture on the upright part of the box (the wall) and continue the theme onto the flat part of the box (the floor). On this flat part use cardboard boxes to create a 3-D display.

Junk sculpture

Using painted card and plastic etc to build upwards – create a stable, junk sculpture with interesting shapes, colours and textures.

Skittles

Paint and decorate old bottles. Fill these with water for stability.

Wall masks

Fold thick paper or thin card and draw half a face outline. Cut a slit for the nose and cut out the eye and mouth. Open out and finish the face with felt tip pens and scraps. Keep the fold for the 3-D mask when mounting on the wall.

Jigsaw

Paint or glue a picture (to please a small child) onto thick card. Use a black felt tip to draw on jigsaw pieces. Cut out.

Puppets

The children paint a character, and stick this onto a piece of card. Cut round the character, and glue a stick to the card.

Classroom or assembly display

Wall masks, framed pictures, junk pictures and fans could depict flora or fauna. Mounted on black papers these would create a stunning environmental classroom or assembly display.

PICTURE ACTIVITY

My Neighbourhood
The built environment

Introduction

The assembly leader introduces the theme: to appreciate, conserve and enhance the amenities and the flora and fauna in the built environment.

Story

The assembly leader says: "Our story today is about the damage to plants and animals from litter pollution." The story *Litter Lesson* could be read by the teacher or one of the children.

Song

Select a suitable song or hymn. For example:

Milk Bottle Tops and Paper Bags
Page 17 in *Someone's Singing, Lord* (A&C Black)
The Building Song
Page 59 in *Hallelujah* (A&C Black)
God bless the grass that grows through the crack
In *Someone's Singing, Lord* (A&C Black)

Poem

Select a suitable poem. For example:

Pollution
In *Tinderbox Assembly Book* (A&C Black)
Windowboxes
In *Poetry Plus – Green Earth and Silver Stars* (Schofield and Sims)
The Dustbin Men
In *A First Poetry Book* (OUP)

Quiet reflection or prayer

For a universal, humanistic or multi-faith assembly:

Quiet reflection

The assembly leader says:

Think about how Shandy was hurt and about all the dangers of litter (pause). At first Jack's mum says Jack is a litter lout. Resolve not to be one yourself (pause). Decide to pick up at least one piece of litter today.

Or for Christian schools:

Prayer

Dear Heavenly Father,

Thank you for beautiful buildings, for gardens, for the flora and fauna in the urban environment. Help us to appreciate, protect and enhance our environment, wherever that may be.

Amen

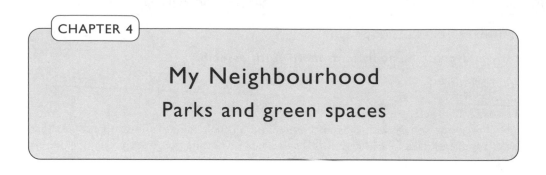

CHAPTER 4

My Neighbourhood
Parks and green spaces

Theme Four: My Neighbourhood: parks and green spaces

Within our urban environments there are parks and green spaces. These could simply be patches of wasteland or a small conservation area. Parks and green spaces are home to a wide variety of species including birds, bats, foxes, squirrels, moths and butterflies.

Environmental Values

- Appreciation: Appreciation of the flora and fauna in parks and green spaces.
- Conservation: Conserving creatures and habitats in the parks and green spaces.
- Protection and enhancement: Valuing biodiversity in parks and green spaces.

A Suggested Lesson Plan

1 Introduce the theme

Green spaces are important for humans and other animals alike. They provide us with habitats for a variety of species, and places for us to appreciate the beauties and wonders of nature. Green spaces can be a place for us to go for quiet reflection and to get away from the daily stresses of modern life. They provide an introduction for children to biodiversity, the cycles of life, and the importance and value of different species.

2 Vocabulary

The teacher ensures that the children understand the words given.

3 The story

The teacher shows the illustration and reads the story.

4 **Talking about the story**

The teacher uses some of the questions and discussion points given, stimulating the children to talk about the story/theme.

5 **Learning activities**

The story activities encourage listening and discussion skills. Follow up activities introduce environmental appreciation and understanding of the natural world as the children explore the environment beyond their homes and gardens. Continuing the themes of biodiversity and respect for the natural world, the learning activities will encourage the children to see parks and green spaces as an extension to the classroom.

1   INTRODUCE THE THEME

Parks and green spaces are an important part of the urban landscape, giving us natural settings to enjoy and places where we can go to relax, or to socialise, and also to learn about many different aspects of nature.

To enjoy parks, woodland, meadows and other green spaces is beneficial to human health. Being close to nature reminds us of our own place in the world, and allows us to marvel at and appreciate the beauty of nature.

Studying and observing the many diverse species of flora and fauna is fascinating, and provides teachers and children alike with a wide range of cross-curricular activities that can be undertaken.

2   VOCABULARY

Story vocabulary

Lurked	–	lying in wait
Leverets	–	young hares
Hesitating	–	waiting nervously
Inquisitively	–	curiously
Petition	–	a list of signatures

Associated environmental vocabulary

Lagomorphs	–	hares and rabbits
Woodland	–	wooded country
Forest	–	large area of trees and undergrowth

Leaps and Bounds

© Mal Leicester, Denise Taylor, Taryn Shrigley-Wightman, Routledge 2009

Leaps and Bounds

Erin and Sam were on their way home from school, and were taking a short cut across Cloudberry Farm and through Bluebell Wood.

Erin grabbed hold of Sam's arm and pulled him to a standstill. "Look!" she whispered, pointing across the field.

Among the grasses and wild flowers, three hares chased each other round and round, leaping high into the air to avoid being caught. They were unaware of the children watching them.

Erin and Sam stood very still. "They're so beautiful," whispered Erin.

The hares suddenly stopped, and looked over to them. They came closer to investigate. Erin and Sam could hardly breathe. If they moved now, they would scare them away. Inquisitively, the hares hopped closer and closer until they were just a few feet away.

"Wow!" said Sam, unable to keep quiet any longer.

The hares, startled by the noise, bounded away and disappeared back into the woods.

Excited by their encounter with the hares, Erin and Sam ran home to tell their mother.

Jackson was the youngest of the three hares seen by the children. He was just discovering the joys of the late spring with his sisters Mirabel and Clara. They danced through Bluebell Wood, as the sun was setting, jumping over fallen tree branches, and chasing each other through the flowers and grasses. The weather was getting warmer, and the birds were busy building nests in the tree tops.

One afternoon, as they were playing at the edge of Bluebell Wood, their mother gave a shrill cry. Suddenly the sky darkened and a large shadow passed over them. The buzzard flew silently and it was lucky that they were still playing in among the trees. Their mother had told them about the many dangers that lurked in the meadows and fields, but the young leverets just loved to run as fast as they could, leaping and bounding, that they paid no attention to her warnings.

As Bluebell Wood grew darker, the night creatures started to come out to play. Fox emerged from his lair, and sniffed the air, and wondered how many tasty rabbits he could catch tonight to feed his hungry cubs.

The moon was high in the sky when Fox paid his nightly visit to the Rabbit Warren in the lee. A large rabbit saw him and started thumping the ground loudly with his hind legs, alerting all the other rabbits. Fox had all night. He settled himself down into a hollow at the base of a large oak tree. He sat and waited, and waited, and waited some more. . . .

Jackson and his sisters gambolled along without a care in the world. *Where were all the rabbits?* they wondered. Bluebell Wood fell silent. A large shape leapt out of the dark, and landed on Clara. She shrieked, and kicked her legs. Realising what was happening, Jackson and Mirabel ran to help their sister. Mirabel was big and strong. She stood tall on her long hind legs and boxed Fox around the ears, nose and head. He let go of Clara and ran off into the bushes. Clara flopped down to the floor, breathing heavily.

"Phew, that was close," said Jackson, his voice trembling. His sisters looked at him with wide eyes. "Let's go home," they cried in unison.

That night they lay low, huddled together, jumping at every noise in the wood. Owls hooted, rabbits screeched, and they could hear Fox barking.

As the sun rose and shone brightly through the trees, the world seemed a brighter place. There were no dark hiding places for Fox in the daylight. The young leverets forgot their fears and gambolled through the bluebells and wild primroses. They raced each other to the edge of Bluebell Wood and back several times. Mirabel was bigger than the others and had long legs. She won each time.

"Look at me," she boasted, kicking her legs high into the air as she ran.

"Mirabel! Be careful," shouted Jackson, as she ran beyond the wood and out into the farmer's field.

"It's fine," cried Mirabel, leaping and bounding even more. "Come on. Race you to the other side."

"No, it's too dangerous. Come back," cried Jackson. "Mother will be angry."

Mirabel paid no heed to her brother. She continued running and leaping and soon she was in the middle of the field.

She seemed to be having so much fun. Jackson and Clara were jealous of their sister, and wanted to have fun too. Hesitating at first, they hopped into the field. Feeling braver, Clara skipped and jumped and boxed her brother on the ear playfully.

"Catch me if you can," she called, and ran away.

Before long the three hares were racing all over the field, chasing each other, and once again they forgot their fears.

". . . . And in the local news today, residents of Pickton gathered outside the Town Hall to protest against the development of a new eco town. Residents are concerned that Bluebell Wood will be destroyed . . ."

"Mum, why are they going to destroy Bluebell Wood?" Erin asked. She glanced across at Sam with a worried look on her face. They were having breakfast, before setting off for school.

"To make way for a new town," said their mother. "We need more houses, and I guess they've chosen this area to build them."

"But where will the hares and all the other creatures live?" asked Sam.

"Oh, don't worry darling, they will find new homes."

Erin and Sam didn't seem convinced by this. How would the hares find new homes? They belonged in Bluebell Wood.

On the way to school, Erin and Sam were unhappy. As they crossed the field by Bluebell Wood, all the animals were busily going about their day. They heard a woodpecker in the distance, and the cry of a buzzard far overhead.

"It's just not fair," said Sam. "They can't just dig up all the trees. What can we do to stop them?"

Later, in their Geography lesson, they told their teacher, Mrs Kettle, about the upsetting news. She listened to everything they had to say with a serious look on her face, and sat thinking for a while.

"I know," she said. "Let's get everyone in the school to sign a petition. Maybe even parents could sign it too. If we get enough signatures, and give the petition to the Council, it might make them change their minds."

"What a brilliant idea," cried Erin, excitedly.

The next morning Mrs Kettle told the rest of the class about the petition to save Bluebell Wood. "I've also told the headteacher, and all the other teachers. Everyone agrees that it's a good idea."

In class later that day, the children all wrote their own letters asking the Council not to destroy Bluebell Wood, and they all took a sheet of lined paper home with them for their parents to sign. A week later, Mrs Kettle gathered all the letters together and the petition. She counted 3,156 signatures, and there were 378 letters. Would it be enough to make a difference?

Erin and Sam were chosen to deliver the petition to the Town Hall, with Mrs Kettle, and they had contacted the local newspaper and radio and TV stations to go along with them.

Later that evening, the news was shown on Midlands Today, and there were Erin and Sam on the telly.

"Well done both of you," said their mother proudly. "Fingers crossed that it works."

"... and in the local news today ... The residents of Pickton claimed a victory after an emergency meeting was held at the Town Hall. The council has decided unanimously that the new town should not be built in this area, and have refused planning permission to the developers ..."

"Hurrah!" shouted Erin and Sam, and hugged each other.

Their mother smiled proudly. "Your three little hares will keep their home, and all thanks to you."

The next day as they walked to school across the field and past Bluebell Wood, three young hares suddenly darted out from among the trees towards them, chasing each other. When they saw the children, they stopped, stood on their hind legs, and watched as the children walked slowly by before carrying on with their game.

4 TALKING ABOUT THE STORY

- What frightened the hares as they played in the woods?
- Why did the developers want to build a new eco town?
- How did the children help to save Bluebell Wood?
- Why is it important to protect our woodlands?

Points for discussion

- Hares look just like rabbits, but are much rarer to spot in the countryside or parks. Discuss with the children the ecology and biology of lagomorphs and their different ways of living. For example, rabbits live in burrows, whilst hares sleep during the day in depressions in the ground.
- Discuss the threats to hares and other species that live on farmland. They are preyed on by foxes, hunted by humans, and they have their habitats disturbed or destroyed through farming practices or development for new towns.

5 LEARNING ACTIVITIES

Appreciation

Humans need green spaces for their wellbeing. For children it is an opportunity for imaginative play in a natural setting where they can observe and interact with a variety of species. Simple activities such as feeding the ducks, swans and geese give children and adults alike a great deal of pleasure. Collecting pine cones and conkers are also favourite activities of young children. Parks and green spaces offer facilities for playing a variety of sports, encourage healthier lifestyles, as well as being a perfect place for quiet reflection.

Arrange an outing to the park or a local nature reserve with the class. The Field Studies Council has a wide range of guides for identifying plants and animals. These can be obtained from www.field-studies-council.org. Alternatively, you can use nature books for species identification.

Encourage the children to use their five senses to explore different colours, smells, and textures of a variety of plants and trees. Take care not to touch any poisonous plants such as Foxgloves (*Digitalis*).

Conservation

Parks and green spaces are usually managed by people. Parks are tended by gardeners who look after the plants, trees and animals. Conservation areas can be created and made into green spaces in an urban setting, and attract many different species of birds, small mammals and insects. Larger mammals such as foxes can also make use of green spaces to live.

Tremendous trees

Trees are often described as being the "lungs of the planet". They come in all shapes and sizes and provide us with food, shelter, and fuel. They are home to many different creatures and birds. Walking in a woodland, forest or glade promotes a sense of wellbeing, and the sound of the wind in a tree's leaves can be soothing. There are some amazing trees throughout the world that are either very old or very tall.

The children can undertake a number of different activities using trees as the main topic:

Tree identification
Using field study guides, the children can try to identify trees in their local parks and green spaces. How many different types of species are there? Which are indigenous to the UK? How old do they think the trees are? Which trees are deciduous and which are evergreen? A simple way to estimate a tree's age is to measure the circumference (distance round) of the trunk at a point 1.5m (5ft) above the ground. Divide the circumference by 2.5 to get the tree's age in years.

Leaf prints
Gather a selection of leaves with different shapes, sizes and textures. Place the individual leaves on a smooth surface and cover with a thin piece of white paper. Using a wax crayon or soft pencil, rub over the leaf. This should produce a picture of the leaf, showing the veins, and other features of the leaf. A similar process can be used for the bark of trees. Place the paper directly onto the bark on a tree, and rub the paper with a wax crayon.

Freshwater conservation

Ponds and streams are home to many different plants and animals. Pond dipping is a traditional activity and great fun for children and adults alike, and is simple to carry out with basic tools and equipment. Field study guides will help to identify the creatures that inhabit our ponds and streams. Some of them are very unusual creatures and look as though they might come from another planet. Discuss the features of the creatures, how they survive in their watery environment, and the various stages of their life cycles. Discuss the creatures that start their early life cycles in water, such as dragonfly larvae, and which emerge onto land later. How do they adapt to the different environments?

Discuss the links with Chapter 6 of this book on the seaside environment and water conservation.

Protection and enhancement

Increasing urbanisation is a threat to our parks and green spaces. The need to build more houses and factories uses land. This can lead to humans and wildlife competing for green space.

It is important for us to protect our parks and green spaces from threats. Pollution, litter, and urban development all put pressures on wildlife habitats.

Protecting biodiversity

Each county in the UK has a local Biodiversity Action Plan (BAP) which looks at land use in urban and rural areas, and what is being done to protect the flora and fauna. Obtain a copy of your local BAP. What are the key concerns or issues in your county? What can the children do to help protect and enhance their local parks and green spaces? Could your class become involved in species surveys, for example? What about writing to your local MP about the concerns of the children? (see Chapter 5 of this book for an example of this activity).

Picture activity

Give each child a photocopy of the picture provided. Use this as a springboard into creative writing – a poem, a description or story. And/or for a research project, using the school library, the bulk library loan and IT suite, how much can the children find out about swans and/or thistles?

Additional learning activities

- Let the children create a word search using the names of animals and plants that can be found in parks and green spaces. The children can complete the word search on the photocopiable page, and use this as an example to develop their own.
- The story in this chapter is about three hares. An ancient motif depicting three hares chasing each other in a circle shows that each hare has two ears, but there are only three ears in the picture. This is believed to be an early puzzle. The motif itself can be traced to China and the Silk Road routes and can be seen in many ancient churches, especially in the south of England. Obtain a picture of the three hares motif (these are readily available from the internet using a simple search on "three hares"). Discuss the properties of the puzzle with the children. Research the history of the three hares in more detail, and the symbolism that is represented in religious customs.

Continued . . .

WORD SEARCH – ANIMALS IN THE PARK

A	X	I	D	F	F	M	C	P	G	D
N	Z	C	H	A	R	E	M	T	R	T
T	C	Y	E	H	O	O	X	M	A	E
R	L	L	O	T	G	E	G	A	S	E
S	J	F	X	E	Y	F	T	G	S	T
Q	F	R	T	O	A	D	D	P	H	G
U	B	E	L	E	Z	E	I	I	O	I
B	W	T	L	J	F	D	D	E	P	D
T	A	T	H	Z	E	E	F	L	P	S
S	Q	U	I	R	R	E	L	O	E	H
C	L	B	E	E	W	T	Y	N	R	E

How many creatures can you find?

Ant

Bee

Butterfly

Frog

Grasshopper

Hare

Magpie

Spider

Squirrel

Toad

PICTURE ACTIVITY

PICTURE ACTIVITY

My Neighbourhood
Parks and green spaces

Theme: Protecting and enjoying parks and green spaces

Introduction

The assembly leader introduces the theme and talks about our wonder and awe at creation and the beauty of the natural world and why we should look after our parks and green spaces.

Give examples of this, such as not leaving litter in the park and writing to your MP to protect green spaces and the creatures that live there.

Story

The assembly leader reminds the children that parks and green spaces can be ideal habitats for lots of different creatures and we can help them by looking after the habitats. Remind the children to take their litter home with them, and not to harm any animals or plants they come across in the park.

The assembly leader or one of the children can read the story *Leaps and Bounds*.

Alternatively, the children could read one or more of their own nature stories, or some of the information they researched about the birds, butterflies, bees and other insects and small mammals that live in parks and green spaces.

Song

Select a song which is relevant to the theme or which echoes the story in some way.

Examples:

Over the Earth is a Mat of Green
In *Someone's Singing, Lord* (A&C Black)

Little Birds in Winter Time
In *Someone's Singing, Lord* (A&C Black)

All Things Which Live Below the Sky
In *Someone's Singing, Lord* (A&C Black)

Poem

Select a suitable poem. Alternatively, you can have a child (or children) read the poems they chose in class. Additionally, some of the children could read their descriptions of their favourite creatures which share their homes.

Quiet reflection or prayer

For a universal, humanistic or multi-faith assembly:

The assembly leader says:
Think of the parks and green spaces you have visited (pause). Picture some of the good times you enjoyed there (pause). Think of one thing you could do to help keep these green spaces looking good.

Or for Christian schools:

Let us pray.

Dear God,

Thank you for our parks and all the animals and plants that live there. Let us be truly grateful for all the energy we have to explore and play in these green spaces.

Amen.

CHAPTER 5

The Countryside

Theme Five: The Countryside

Children who live in the countryside can learn to appreciate and protect their environment. Urban children can also learn to appreciate and enjoy the countryside and understand why its conservation enhances the lives of humans and animals. Much of the countryside is farmland and we depend upon this for much of our food.

Environmental Values

- Appreciation: Appreciation of the countryside and its flora and fauna.
- Conservation: Protecting plants and creatures and their habitats and ecosystems. It is important that farmland contains areas for wildlife to flourish such as hedgerows and buffer zones, and that chemicals used are not harmful.
- Protection and enhancement: planting, creating wildlife havens.

A Suggested Lesson Plan

1 **Introduce the theme**

The countryside is the home of trees, plants and a diversity of creatures. We can appreciate and enjoy the beauty of the countryside – its mountains, forests, trees, rivers and lakes, and its many wild creatures. How can we conserve and enhance all these natural gifts?

2 **Vocabulary**

The teacher ensures that the children understand the words given.

3 **The story**

The teacher shows the illustration and reads the story.

4   **Talking about the story**

The teacher uses some of the questions and discussion points given, stimulating the children to talk about the story/theme.

5   **Learning activities**

The story activities encourage listening and discussion skills. Follow-up activities develop appreciation, knowledge and understanding of the countryside and its wild flora and fauna.

1   INTRODUCE THE THEME

- The countryside with its beauty, peace and fresh air is invaluable and must be protected.
- The trees and plants provide the oxygen we need.
- The countryside provides habitats for many wild creatures.

2   VOCABULARY

Story vocabulary

Wretched	–	*unhappy*
Scowled	–	*frowned*
Retrieved	–	*brought back*
Glinted	–	*gave off gleams of light*
Shimmering	–	*giving off waves of light*
Grateful	–	*thankful*
Moored-up	–	*secured the boat at rest*
Avoiding	–	*keeping away from*
Struggled	–	*fought*
Snuffling	–	*sniffing*

Associated environmental vocabulary

Farm land	–	*land used by farmers to grow crops or to keep livestock*
Agricultural	–	*farming*
Wild creatures	–	*animals in the wild, independent of people; not domestic*
Wild flowers	–	*flowers that grow in the wild – not planted and tended by people*
Chemical pollutants	–	*substances which contaminate the environment*
Photosynthesis	–	*the process in which trees and other green plants take in carbon dioxide and give out oxygen*

Down the Canal

Down the Canal

It was my birthday and the sun was shining but I was wretched, totally down. I scowled at the opened parcels on my bed.

"Happy birthday darling," said Mum from the doorway.

I turned my scowl on her. "What about my mobile phone?" I said.

"I told you Emily, that will be when you're older. Next year maybe."

"But I thought you were kidding me," I wailed. "For a surprise!"

Mum sighed and went downstairs. I sat on my bed and felt like crying. Pepper, my retriever dog, came and put his heavy head on my lap to comfort me. His big brown eyes looked up and I stroked his yellow fur.

"It's not fair Pepper," I said. "Nearly everyone in my class has one already."

We were just finishing breakfast when all our relatives arrived. Dad had hired a canal boat for the day as my birthday treat. I began to cheer up until my cousin Lauren came in.

"Look Emily. Dad got this as a freebie and he's given it to me. Isn't it cool?"

In her hand was a totally fabulous black and silver mobile phone. And she's a whole year younger than me. And it wasn't even her birthday. I turned away. I just couldn't manage to say anything.

On the canal boat I kept as far away from Lauren as I could. She kept coming over and each time I moved away. She looked puzzled and sad. I didn't care. In fact I was glad. I didn't talk to any of them, didn't join in their silly chatter or laugh at their silly jokes.

I just watched the bank slide by as our boat sailed over the water.

It was an autumn day. The leaves on the trees were red and gold, and sunlight glinted on the river. There were silver fish in the water, blue dragonflies shimmering above it and cows, sheep and horses in the fields. Swans glided by and a duck with her whole family of the sweetest, tiny babies swam near the boat. In spite of myself, I began to feel better. It was so beautiful on the water. My bad feelings came back though when from the end of the boat I heard Lauren's phone ring.

We were coming up to a lock and Dad and Uncle Tom worked the lock gates.

"Put Pepper inside," Dad told me.

"I'll hold him Dad," I promised.

"I said, he goes inside." Dad stressed each word.

"Huh," I said, but I had to take Pepper into the cabin.

Everyone else was at the lock or on the deck watching as Dad motored our boat through the gates. I couldn't bear to leave Pepper on his own, so, as the water drained down, all I could see was the lock walls sliding by. What a birthday this was turning out to be! Pepper was grateful though, and there in our slimy stone prison, he licked my face in a sloppy wet kiss.

At lunchtime we moored up by a place with a small lake and picnic tables under the trees. We crunched through the leaves and unloaded the picnic. I was still avoiding Lauren, not even looking at her, but I did look over to her table when she yelled out,

"My phone, I've lost my phone."

I felt a sneaking little dart of pleasure and tried hard not to smile. Several people got out their own phones to dial her number.

"I turned it off to save my battery," she said, and I must confess, I did smile at that.

Then I had an idea. I thought I knew how I might be able to find Lauren's phone.

But should I try? For several moments the good and bad sides of me struggled inside my head. I didn't want Lauren to have a phone. Even though I knew it was mean, I decided to keep quiet. But then I saw tears in Lauren's eyes and I knew how I would feel in her place. I said, rather unwillingly, "Give me your glove Lauren."

Looking puzzled Lauren handed me her red glove. I held it to Pepper's nose and he sniffed it.

"Find, Pepper!" I said. "Find, boy!"

And my dog went snuffling in the leaves until he suddenly pushed his nose in deeper and came up with Lauren's phone in his mouth. Everyone cheered as Pepper brought the phone and placed it at my feet. I picked it up and handed it to Lauren.

She smiled at me and I smiled back.

My bad feelings hadn't completely disappeared but they had sunk down like the water in the lock.

On the journey back I felt better and better. I love creatures. We counted twenty-five different kinds. We had a great afternoon, Lauren and I.

And as Pepper's reward, Dad let me have him out of the boat on a lead to watch the boat going back up the locks.

By the end of the journey I no longer minded about the phone. In any case, what's having a mobile phone anyway, compared with owning the so totally greatest, most brilliant dog in the World?

4   TALKING ABOUT THE STORY

- Why did Emily feel like crying on her birthday?
- Name some of the creatures Emily saw on her canal trip.
- How did Pepper find Lauren's mobile phone?
- What does Emily realise in the end?

Points for discussion

- Who knows how canal locks work?
- Why does Emily keep away from Lauren? (She is envious of her mobile phone.)
  How does envy feel? What is the difference between envy and jealousy? (We are
  envious of things – the belongings of others. We are jealous of people – perhaps
  getting more attention than we are, or having more success.) How can we help
  ourselves to feel less envious or jealous? (for example: appreciate what we have; try
  to like other people and have good wishes for them).

  - Why are canals good for the environment?
    They provide an excellent habitat for wild flora and fauna.
    Canals could be used more for the transport of goods, as they used to be. We
    would then need fewer lorries with their heavy use of resources of gases and
    their polluting emissions.
    Canals are a natural environment for family recreation.
    Canals reflect a slower pace of life – canal boats are a slow and relaxing way of
    travelling.

5   LEARNING ACTIVITIES

Appreciation

A walk in the country and nature poetry.

A walk in the country

A walk in the country – for urban children a day out for a walk and picnic can be a
memorable experience. For rural schools, the children can be encouraged to learn more
about local flora and fauna. After the walk, discuss with the children why so many writers
and artists use aspects of the countryside in their work. The magic of nature is an
inspiration for artistic expression.

Nature poetry

Read some nature poetry with the children and discuss the poems. There are many
nature poems in poetry anthologies for primary school children. For example:

- *The Young Puffin Book of Verse*, e.g. *Hurt no living thing*
- Poems in the OUP Poetry books (a first, a second, a third, a fourth, a fifth poetry book)
- Poems in *Green Earth and Silver Stars* (Schofield and Sims)
- Poems in *The Squirrel in the Town* (Blackie)

In addition, simple "adult" poems can be introduced. For example, *The Daffodils* by William Wordsworth.

Finally the older children could write their own nature poem and illustrate it with a drawing or painting whilst the younger children could create a painting or picture with labels of the main subjects.

Conservation

Letter to your MP

Writing to your MP about environmental issues is a contribution children can make to the environmental agenda. Show the children how a formal letter is correctly laid out, explain and discuss the differences between local and national government, and discuss what issues are influenced by local councillors and what issues are influenced by your local MP.

Explain to the children that MPs can influence government policy through the votes they make in parliament.

Ask the children to write a letter to their local MP. This should be set out properly, and suggest some specific policies that would help to protect or enhance the countryside and which a local MP could have some influence over.

Protection and enhancement

The importance of trees

Trees are Earth's largest plants! Ask the children why trees are important.

- For photosynthesis – the process whereby trees (and other green plants) take in carbon dioxide and give out oxygen
- For oxygen, which is needed for all air-breathing creatures, including human beings
- For wood
- For food for humans, birds and animals
- They absorb sound
- They are beautiful to look at
- They provide shelter

Show a picture with as many indigenous species of trees as possible. Discuss with the children why trees might disappear. For each reason given, cover one of the trees in the picture. Now divide the alphabet between four or five groups of children. Can each group find a tree that begins with each of their letters? They could draw each of the trees and older children could add some information points (the information could be found in the bulk library loan or using the IT suite).

Feely box

Cover some objects with a cloth. Let the children feel the objects and try to guess what they are. Can they think what links them all (i.e. trees)? Examples of objects: paper, wooden object, fruit, nuts, leaves, acorn, cone, etc.

Picture activity

Give each child a photocopy of the picture provided. Use this as a springboard into creative writing: a poem, description or story. And/or for a research project, using the school library, the bulk library loan and IT suite, how much can the children find out about sheep and/or rowan trees?

Additional learning activities

*   *The Lorax* by Dr Seuss
    The children will enjoy reading this book with you. Discuss all the important environmental messages such as overusing the Earth's resources.
*   Clay model
    The children could choose any wild creature they like. Older children can research more about the behaviour of the creature and its habitat. All the children could make a clay model of their chosen creature, or they could make a model of an imaginary creature. Discuss the food and shelter their imaginary creature would need, given its characteristics.
*   The school garden or a "wild" area (see Chapter 2 for further suggestions)
    Neglected edges could make small borders for the children to cultivate and look after, learning about planting seeds at different depths, etc. A spare piece of neglected ground could be turned into a wild garden, creating habitats for many creatures and the growth of wild flowers and plants.
*   The Countryside Code
    You could look at the website at www.countrysideaccess.gov.uk for many ideas and much information and free education packs and resources. Give the children the photocopiable page *The Country Code*. You (or the children) could write each rule on a Countryside Code Chart for the classroom wall. Discuss each "rule" with the children. Why is it a good idea? To complete the page (and chart), can the children think of other good rules to add? Finally, the children could construct their own "A Town Code" (drawing on earlier chapters such as "The Built Environment") and have the charts side-by-side on the classroom wall.

THE COUNTRYSIDE CODE

- Don't leave litter
- Don't pollute water
- Keep safe (be aware of steep drops, deep or fast running water)
- Guard against fire
- Fasten all gates
- Keep your dogs under control
- Keep to public footpaths across farmland
- Do not pester livestock
- Do not trample crops

-
-
-
-

PICTURE ACTIVITY

PICTURE ACTIVITY

Introduction

The assembly leader introduces the theme: why we should enjoy and protect the countryside and its flora and fauna.

Story

The story could be read by a teacher or child. The story could be *Down the Canal* or a story specially chosen or written by the children which is set in or is about the countryside.

Songs

Select songs which are relevant to the theme or encourage the children to do so. For example:

The World is Such a Lovely Place
No 8 in *Every Colour Under the Sun* (Ward Lock Educational)

Over the Earth is a Mat of Green
No 10 in *Someone's Singing, Lord*, 2nd edition (A&C Black 2002)

Keep the Countryside Tidy
In *Every Colour Under the Sun* (Ward Lock Educational)

Poems

Select a suitable poem. Alternatively, you can have a child (or children) read some of their own nature poems.

Examples of nature poems:

I'm a Tree
Page 93 in *Smile Please* by Tony Bradman (Puffin 1989)

Ten Tall Oak Trees
In *Another Fifth Poetry Book* (OUP)

Up on the Downs
In *A Very First Poetry Book* (OUP)

Quiet reflection

Think about the beauty of the countryside – its forests, mountains, lakes, wild flowers and creatures (pause); imagine a world where cities cover the land – no countryside remaining; think about how bleak and dreary that would be (pause); let us resolve to do what we can to protect our green spaces and our beautiful places (pause).

Christian

Heavenly Father, thank you for the beautiful countryside, for trees, plants, wild flowers, lakes and rivers. Thank you for the wild creatures who live there. Help us to appreciate and protect our wonderful world. Amen.

CHAPTER 6

The Seaside Environment

Theme Six: The Seaside Environment

The seaside is an exciting place for most children, but do be aware that there may be children in the class who have not had this experience. The vivid blue sea is awe inspiring and is great fun for paddling, swimming or sailing. It is home to an amazing diversity of wonderful creatures. It is also fun to make sand castles and play on and with the yellow sand. Rock pools are magical and accessible places. These intrinsic attractions of the beach can readily be used as a way into environmental concerns.

Environmental Values

- Appreciation: Appreciation of the seaside and sea creatures
- Conservation: Water pollution awareness
- Protection and enhancement: Valuing biodiversity in the marine environment

A Suggested Lesson Plan

1 Introduce the theme

At the seaside the land meets the sea. The oceans of the earth comprise 70% of Planet Earth. It is important to appreciate the beauty and environmental importance of the sea and to know and appreciate the diversity of sea creatures. How can we protect this part of our fragile planet?

2 Vocabulary

The teacher ensures that the children understand the words given.

3 The story

The teacher shows the illustration and reads the story.

4 **Talking about the story**

The teacher uses some of the questions and discussion points given, stimulating the children to talk about the story/theme.

5 **Learning activities**

The story activities encourage listening and discussion skills. Follow up activities introduce environmental appreciation and understanding in a marine context.

1 INTRODUCE THE THEME

- 70% of Planet Earth is ocean (this is why the Earth is known as the Blue Planet)
- The oceans sustain many different kinds of interesting creatures
- Human life and marine life depend upon human beings not contaminating or over-exploiting (for example by over-fishing) the sea

2 VOCABULARY

Story vocabulary

Simmered	–	*almost boiled*
Spoilt	–	*ruined*
Wasting	–	*not using (unused; destroying)*
Monochrome	–	*one colour*
Copying	–	*mimicking*
Intrigued	–	*curious, interested*
Miniature	–	*on a small scale; small*
Shoal	–	*a group of fish*
Ripple	–	*a small wave on water*
Repetitions	–	*doing or saying again*
Vivid	–	*bright*
Glinted	–	*gleamed*
Translucent	–	*almost see-through*
Commendation	–	*praise; a public award for praiseworthy action*
Solemnity	–	*seriousness*

Associated environmental vocabulary

Rockpool	—	*seawater trapped in rocks making a small habitat*
Shells	—	*the hard outer covering of a shellfish*
Anemone	—	*a sea creature attached to rock or other hard surface*
Lichens	—	*a plant (consisting of a fungus and an algae) forming crusts and tufts on stones, trees and soil*
Sea creatures	—	*animals who live in sea water*
Water pollution	—	*to dirty or contaminate water (rivers, lakes, oceans, etc), making it harmful to humans and/or creatures and/or plants.*
water cycles	—	*a series of water changes in a fixed order, repeating itself*

Another World

Another World

It was the last day of term and in our hot classroom, excitement simmered like a stew.

"Cool no school," came a loud whisper and we all laughed, even Mrs Singh.

"Well cool down now," she said. She held up a Better Books catalogue. "They are having a writing competition for the holiday. The winner gets five hundred pounds and five hundred pounds for their school library."

"Huh," Emily whispered in my ear "Why should school get half anyway?"

I've never won a competition but my sister Erica is always winning things and being chuffed and having everyone say well done.

"I'd love to win," I whispered back.

"Stop whispering you two," said Mrs Singh. "Becs, take one of these entry forms. You're quite good at writing."

That evening I told Mum about the competition.

"I'm already eight and you have to be between eight and eleven and write five hundred words max, on *Another World*. Miss said I was quite good at writing and I've promised her I'll have a go. She's given me two entry forms in case I spoil one."

"You'll be wasting your time," said Erica, who was doing her homework at the kitchen table. "*Quite* good just isn't good enough to win."

"She might," said Mum. "Anyway having a go is what counts."

"Well I could have a go too. I'm not twelve yet. I'll have your spare entry form Becs, and I do have a good chance!"

I felt my bubble of hope and excitement burst into nothing. I had no chance against Erica.

Mum put her arm around my shoulders and gave me a squeeze.

"Do your best Becs, you never know."

I nodded. I had promised Mrs Singh so all I could do was my best.

Five weeks later Emily was helping me to plant seeds. I have a little plot of my own in our garden and I try to keep some colour there all the year round.

"Have you done your competition entry yet?" she asked me.

I shook my head. "I can't think what to write about. I've tried and tried. I thought about the moon but Erica has written about *Monochrome Mars*. She says I'll be copying her if I write about another planet. Even the moon."

"She would," said Emily indignantly. "What other worlds are there? Anyway, is her Mars thing any good?"

"It's brilliant," I said.

We worked in silence for a while.

"We go to Pembrokeshire next week. Then it's back to school. I'm running out of time Emily. I just wish I had an idea. It's not that I'd win but at least I'd keep my promise to Mrs Singh. She's sure to ask me what I did."

It was our first day in Pembrokeshire and Erica asked if I'd done my piece yet. I shook my head and she grinned.

"Why not do the moon after all?" said Mum.

"And copy my idea," sniffed Erica.

"The moon is not copying Mars," said Dad sharply.

Erica sneered at me behind his back.

"Anyway loads of kids will choose the moon Dad. I want to do something a bit different," I said.

"More original," said Mum.

"Yeah right," said Erica, in her most irritating sarcastic voice.

That night I couldn't get to sleep. I tossed and turned and tried to think of another world I could write about. I thought of writing a story, but those I thought of were all about space travel to other planets. Perhaps I could write one about travelling back in time or forward to the future? That would be like visiting another world, but on this planet. The trouble was my history wasn't that good for the past or my science for the future!

The next day we met up on the beach with some friends of Mum and Dad and their son Lewis. Lewis was my age and he was nice.

"Shall we go and look at the rock pools?" he asked me and Erica.

"I've already seen them," Erica said, in her superior way.

"I can never see them too much," Lewis said. "You always see something new."

Erica shrugged but I was intrigued and went with him. They weren't far away, several rock pools in a stretch of grey rocks at the edge of the beach. We stopped at the first one and looked in. I liked the miniature seaweed garden waving in the clear water but I didn't see much else until Lewis began to point out the creatures.

"Look," he said, pointing to a shoal of tiny fishes. I saw them swirling about like specks of living silver.

"Wow," said Lewis, "a sand fish."

He pointed and I saw a small patch of sand in the shape of a tiny fish rise up and ripple across the bottom of the pond, settling back and disappearing again against the sandy rock. I began to notice other things then – the pretty shells, a tiny waving anemone and the tiny crabs. They more we looked the more we saw. Limpets, lichens, almost invisible prawns, starfish, worms.

"It's magical," I said. "I've never really noticed before. The more you look the more you see."

"And the more you know how to look," Lewis said. "It's really a world of its own."

"Another world," I shouted, making him jump.

"Sorry," I said, and I explained about the competition. "And you see," I finished "a rock pool is another world, a world within our world."

"It's a great idea," Lewis said, "and I've got a rock pool book that you can borrow so you get the right names."

I borrowed Lewis's book and that evening I wrote my piece. It came out too long but I cut out unnecessary words and repetitions and it made it better. The next night I re-read the piece and re-wrote a poor sentence. I remembered what Mrs Singh had said about vivid verbs and adjectives and changed swam to rippled and shone to glinted and see-through to translucent. I really tried my hardest but I wasn't really sure. Would a rock pool count as another world? And would anyone but me and Lewis think they were magical? Anyway, the next day I posted it. Only two days before the deadline! Back at school Mrs Singh was pleased that I had sent in an entry.

"A rock pool," she said in surprise. "I think most people will write about the planets."

After that I forgot about the competition, though I continued to read about rock pools and then about creatures in the sea. In fact I chose sea creatures for my topic work. Four weeks later two letters plopped through our letterbox. One was for Erica and one was for me. Erica opened hers.

"I've got a commendation for my *Monochrome Mars*," she said, waving the piece of paper triumphantly.

"Well done," we all said, me and Mum and Dad.

"Perhaps you'll have a commendation too, Becs," said Mum.

Erica smirked. "It's probably just to say you haven't been successful. They do that."

"Well open up your letter Becs," said Dad.

Three pairs of eyes watched me as I did so. I drew out the letter, longing for my own commendation. What I read there made me punch the air. "Yes!"

I was grinning fit to split my face in two as I read out the first few lines:

"Dear Rebecca Bennett,
We are delighted to inform you that your piece about rock pools has
*won the Better Reads **Another World** writing competition."*

"But a rock pool isn't another world," Erica interrupted. "That's not fair."

"That's exactly what a rock pool is, I reckon," said Dad. "Anyway, Erica, be a good sport."

Erica took a deep breath. "Well done Becs," she said.

She held out her hand and we shook rather solemnly.

"Thanks," I said.

I was very happy and it wasn't really the winning or even the money that was making me glow inside. It wasn't even that my piece would be published. It was suddenly knowing that I really had created something good in the end.

4   TALKING ABOUT THE STORY

- Why were the children excited (at the beginning of the story)?
- How did Erica get an entry form for the competition?
- What ideas did Becs have that she couldn't use? Why not?
- What did Becs do to improve her piece?
- Why was Becs really happy in the end?

Points for discussion

- Why did Becs want to win a competition? (what is sibling rivalry?)
- In what ways is a rock pool like another world?
- Why does a rock pool seem magical?
- Name some other wonderful things in the natural world.

5   LEARNING ACTIVITIES

Appreciation

Using our senses

We use our five senses to find out about the world – sight, sound, smell, touch, taste. How do we know what is in a rock pool? We look very carefully and we know what kinds of things to look for.

1. We see the waving green seaweed, the coloured stones and shells, the tiny glinting silver fish, etc.
2. We hear the waves breaking nearby
3. We smell the briny seaside scents
4. We touch rough rock and grainy sand
5. We taste the salty sea

Think of some other wonderful place or object in nature (example rainbows, butterflies, snowflakes, forest, waterfalls, seahorses). Make a list of the wonderful places and natural objects or natural wonders which the children suggest. The children can do a painting of one of these wonderful places, seeking to remember that if they were in that situation there would be things to see, to hear, to touch. They should try to make their painting vivid and to capture that sense of wonder. Next the children should write a description of their place, imagining they are there and bringing in what they see, what they hear, what they smell, what they feel, what they touch, what they taste. Finally the children can use their description as the setting for a story of their own.

Conservation

Becs and Lewis like the rock pool. They would never spoil it by polluting it or removing the creatures, plants or stones. Make a classroom environmental chart. For the top half, discuss how to conserve our seaside and write down some simple rules and ideas on the chart. For example, no litter on the beach or in the sea, no polluting rock pools, no over-fishing, no oil in the sea. This could be placed next to the classroom environmental poster completed in Chapter 4. In the bottom half of the sheet, cut rounded corners to make a rock pool shape, have a pale blue background, and then each child can draw or paint a rock pool plant or creature, and glue it onto the rock pool half of the chart.

Protection and enhancement

Water use

We all use far more water than we realise. For example, our washing machine uses about 65 litres for each wash, flushing the toilet uses 8 litres, taking a bath uses about 80 litres, and taking a shower about 35 litres. Each person in Britain uses about 155 litres per day. A person in sub-Saharan Africa uses approximately 20 litres per day. (How much more water do you use each day than a child in Africa?)

Think of ways we could save water. Ask the children to try to think of five good ideas. Examples could include:

* Sometimes take a shower instead of a bath.
* Do not let the tap run while you are brushing your teeth.
* Water the garden with water that has already been used for washing dishes.
* Collect rain water for the garden in a water butt.

Picture activity

Give each child a photocopy of the pictures provided. Use this as a springboard into creative writing: a poem, description or story. And/or for a research project, using the school library, the bulk library loan and IT suite, how much can the children find out about dolphins and/or sea mosses and seaweed?

Additional learning activities

World of colour

Let each child choose another wonderful place from their brainstormed list of wonderful places. Now they should draw that place in black and white and draw it again in vivid colour. How much we gain from a world of colour!

Make a rock pool

Use a large plastic bowl. The children make rock pool creatures and objects and place them in the bowl. For example: use silver foil for fish, and colourful small shells and stones, use painted straws for sand worms, buttons for anemones, plasticine or clay to make creatures, painted string for seaweed, and paint eyes onto stones for bottom-dwelling fish. Cover with cling film to look like shining water.

Exciting reading

Devote some class reading time to one of the wonderful books about sea journeys, pirates or treasure islands. A further original rock pool story is also provided courtesy of LCP Publishers, Leamington Spa.

Water cycle story

Tell the children: Imagine you are a drop of water in the sea. You are evaporated into water vapour, blown up to the sky by the wind, and become part of a cloud. You fall as rain onto water (sea, lake, or stream) to become part of the cycle again. Write out your story as a drop of rain. Describe the places you are in, how you feel (warm/cold; exhilarated/frightened; joyful/miserable), and what you meet on the way (creatures in the water). You could have an adventure, provided you complete your journey.

Rebecca's *Another World*

Give the children the photocopiable page of *Another World* by Rebecca Bennett. Together read Rebecca's winning competition entry. Now ask the children to pick out vivid adjectives and strong verbs.

Can they pick out the figures of speech?

Do these figures of speech work? Why/Why not?

Do the children think Rebecca's piece conveys another world?

What do they like and what do they dislike about it?

Finally, ask the children to write their own 500 words (max) on *Another World*.

Another World

By Rebecca Bennett

On many of the sea shores curving round our world, rock pools are left behind by the sea. These small, shallow shines of water are teeming with animals and plants. Each warm, natural aquarium provides a habitat, a welcome haven for its inhabitants. However, they are not without some danger, from predators and from the unwanted fresh water which collects in heavy rain.

Twice a day the blue tide turns, brining new creatures into the rock pools and sweeping others back out to sea. Though some creatures return to the ocean with the very next tide, others move on to larger pools and some remain in the same one all of their lives. Thus each individual pool is a different world, with its own unique and changing mix of life. Diverse and fascinating fish swim there, while worms of various shapes and sizes creep along the rock pool bed and crabs walk up the sides. Translucent stripy prawns dart through the water, flat worms are propelled through it by tiny hairs, and jellyfish gracefully float. Interest, movement and colour are also provided by the seaweed, which, like a miniature garden in the breeze, gently waves in the soft currents. Barnacles, limpets and anemones cling to the rock pool sides. Variously coloured shells and stones, like underwater jewels, decorate the ground.

Though rock pools are as open as eyes in the rocks, their contents are like hidden treasure, which you find only by looking carefully and patiently. The more you look into the rock pool the more you will discover.

The first time I looked into a rock pool I saw a tiny fish-shape rise slightly from the sandy bottom of the pool and ripple across some few inches before sinking back down. Its sandy looking back was such good camouflage that once down it was completely undetectable. It disappeared like something in a conjuring trick.

If reflected sunlight makes it difficult to see into the water, make a rock pool viewer. Cut a Perspex sheet to make a round window and attach this, using a waterproof seal, to a pipe with a large diameter. The pipe should be about 30–40 cm long. Push the window end of the viewer into the water, and look down the pipe and through the window, and discover a universe you might have jumped over unaware.

When you know how to look into a rock pool you know how to see *another world* – an enchanting, magical world within our own Planet Earth.

The Rock Pool

Basic story

Dan is on holiday. It is raining and he is bored. He has nothing to do. He tries to make friends with Tom, another boy staying in the same guest house. At first Tom is too shy but later, on the beach, Dan and Tom become friends. They look into a magical rock pool, full of small creatures. They have a great week together. They stay in touch when the holiday is over.

Detailed story

One morning I dreamed I was swimming in the sea with seahorses, but when I woke up the splashing of the waves turned out to be the sound of heavy rain outside. I sighed. At first my holiday had been fun, but now I was missing my friends to play with. The rain would only make things worse. I dressed quickly and went down to the dining room with Mum and Dad.

During breakfast a boy about my own age came in with his parents. They sat at the table next to ours. My Mum smiled at the other Mum.

"Look Dan, someone to play with," she whispered.

From time to time I looked over at the other boy, and when he glanced in our direction, I smiled and raised a hand. He looked down at his plate immediately. I felt angry. He ignored me on purpose!

"How rude was that?" I said to Mum.

"I think maybe he's shy," she said.

The new family left the dining room first.

"Are they here on holiday?" Mum asked our waitress.

"Yes. They came today, just for one week. Room 21. He's very interested in creatures, the young lad. Birds, beasts, fish, even spiders and snakes, according to his Mum." She gave a big pretend shudder and we all grinned.

After breakfast we went into the hotel lounge. We came to the "Seaview" last Saturday and had one more week to go. The truth is, I was bored. Half-heartedly I looked along the hotel's bookcase. There was a whole shelf of books about sea creatures. That gave me an idea.

"I'll tell that boy about these," I said to Mum, "since he likes creatures."

I ran up the stairs to Room 21, hoping the boy would come back down with me. I rapped out three loud knocks on their door, which was opened by his Mum. I leaned forward eagerly.

"There's loads of books about loads of sea creatures downstairs," I told her.

"How kind of you to come and tell us," she said. "Tom will be pleased. Hang on a second would you?"

She disappeared and I could hear talking inside. It sounded almost like a disagreement. She came back to the door on her own.

"He says thank you," she said, smiling at me, and gently she closed the door.

I stared at it. He hadn't even bothered to come to the door! I stamped back down the stairs. With Mum and Dad, I acted like I didn't care, but inside I felt really angry. From now on, I would completely ignore him!

It was a very boring morning. Mum and Dad read the papers and did the crossword together. I had nothing to do, and no-one to do it with, but in the afternoon the rain stopped and we went to the beach. I made a big sandcastle, and was digging out a moat when the new family passed by.

"That's a splendid castle," the boy's Mum said.

The boy nodded in agreement, and, to my surprise, he grinned at me. I stared through him unsmiling and went on with my moat. The truth is, I felt a mean satisfaction that it was me ignoring him this time.

I went to a nearby rock pool to fetch water for my moat. I had just begun to lower my bucket into the pool when the boy appeared and grabbed my arm.

"N . . n . . no. P . . please. D . . . don't d . . disturb . . . creatures . . p . . please!"

"It's their home," his Mum said from just behind him. "Look. See the tiny fishes."

We all stared into the clear water of the rock pool.

"See the seaweed and barnacles and that sea anemone, like a minia-ture garden," said the boy's Dad. "And the little silver fish and tiny crab."

I looked and saw that the rock pool was a small world of its own.

"And that little jellyfish," said the boy's Mum. "And if you look very carefully you can see the prawns darting – they're almost see-through, but with broken brown lines."

"Wow!" said the boy. "A s . . sandfish." He pointed into the pool.

"That sand near the orange Cushion Star," his Dad said to me.

As I watched, a patch of sand in the shape of a broad flat fish rose a little, and with a rippling of its fins, swam across the bottom of the pool. When it settled back down, once more it disappeared, camouflaged against the sand beneath it.

The Story

"Cool!" I said. The boy looked up and smiled at me.

"It's a g . . great r . . rockpool." He said.

Mum was right, I thought. *He is shy. I should have given him more of a chance.* I smiled back.

"I'd never have seen that sandy fish," I said.

"W . . would you like to s . . see a s . . seal?" he asked. I nodded. "I'm Dan by the way."

"T . . Tom," he said.

We all went to see the seals. My Mum and Dad came too. We walked over some rocks overlooking a small bay. The sea was flat and blue. We watched and waited. Suddenly a small head, like a wet sea-dog's head, popped out of the water and two big bright eyes stared at us. Magic!

After that we had a great week, me and Tom. He showed me more sea creatures in other rock pools. And once, we even saw some dolphins leaping in the bay. How could I have been bored with so many amazing creatures to discover? We became good friends, and when Tom got to know me, his stammer, like the sandfish, almost disappeared.

By the end of the week I had changed my mind about going home. I wanted to see my friends, but I was sad I wouldn't see Tom again.

At bedtime on the last night, Mum said, "By the way, Tom's Mum has invited us on a visit, once we're all back home. They live near an Aquatic Centre with seahorses, and sharks, and some amazing tropical fish. We can all go there together."

I felt a huge grin stretch from ear to ear. I snuggled down to sleep, and once more I dreamed of seahorses, and of the bright blue sea.

© Mal Leicester

We are grateful to LCP for permission to reproduce this story, which is published in their cross-curricular files (File: The Beach)

PICTURE ACTIVITY

PICTURE ACTIVITY

The Seaside Environment

Introduction

The assembly leader introduces the theme: to appreciate, conserve and enhance our beautiful coast.

Story

The assembly leader or a child reads a story. This could be:
   Another World or *The Rock Pool* or one of the children's own stories.

Song

Choose an appropriate song or hymn. For example:

The Sun That Shines Across the Sea
In *Someone's Singing, Lord* (A&C Black)

Poem

Select a suitable poem. There are many seaside poems in children's poetry anthologies. For example:

At the Seaside
Page 76 in *Smile Please* (Puffin)

The Sea
Page 68 in *A Very First Poetry Book* (OUP)

Sea Song
Page 69 in *A Very First Poetry Book* (OUP)

Alternatively, a child could read Rebecca's competition entry on *Another World* and some of the children could read their own place descriptions.

Quiet reflection or prayer

For a universal, humanistic or multi-faith assembly:

Quiet Reflection
The assembly leader says: Imagine the vast blue sea and the waves crashing onto the beach. Think of the beauty and power and wonder of the oceans of our fragile blue planet (pause). Think about how the sea becomes polluted and over-fished (pause). Resolve to protect the seaside environment however you can (pause).

Or for Christian schools:

Prayer

Almighty Creator,

Thank you for the wonderful oceans of our world and for all the sea creatures. Help us to appreciate, protect and enhance the seaside environment.

Amen

CHAPTER 7

Countries Far Away

Theme Seven: Countries Far Away

Children have access to information about countries far away through television, books, magazines and the internet or world wide web. They can learn about biodiversity through nature programmes, and about different cultures. We are increasingly aware of the many problems and issues that threaten wildlife and natural habitats, but at the same time we can still appreciate and marvel at the wonders of nature.

Human culture and nature are interlinked. Art has always expressed the human interest in the natural world, and different human societies co-exist with wildlife.

Many of the problems affecting wildlife and natural habitats, however, are also anthropogenic (or human-caused). The increasing human population puts strains and stresses on habitats, ecosystems and many different species of flora and fauna. We need to recognise the damage we are causing, but conserving and protecting wildlife and habitats and co-existing with larger species relies on our understanding, knowledge and respect.

Environmental Values

- Appreciation: Appreciation of diversity, both biological diversity (biodiversity) and cultural diversity.
- Conservation: Conserving biodiversity and cultural diversity.
- Protection and enhancement: Protecting biodiversity and cultural diversity through sustainable development.

A Suggested Lesson Plan

1 **Introduce the theme**

How can we learn to understand and appreciate wildlife and natural habitats on a global scale?

2 **Vocabulary**

The teacher ensures that the children understand the words given.

3 **The story**

The teacher shows the illustration and reads the story.

4 **Talking about the story**

The teacher uses some of the questions and discussion points given, stimulating the children to talk about the story/theme.

5 **Learning activities**

The story activities encourage listening and discussion skills. Follow-up activities introduce environmental appreciation and understanding of the natural world in a global context. Looking at countries far away, the children will be encouraged to appreciate the importance of humans co-existing with wildlife and natural habitats, and to minimise the impact humans have. Human culture is closely interlinked with nature, and art has expressed the human fascination with nature since the early cave paintings thousands of years ago. Tolerance, respect and co-existence in an increasingly modern world are more important today than at any other time in history.

1 **INTRODUCE THE THEME**

- Understanding the different aspects of countries, their ecosystems and natural habitats, and wildlife.
- Understanding co-existence with other species of animals, and also with other human societies and cultures.
- Recognising the problems that other countries face and the various threats to wildlife and natural habitats, and how we can help to minimise these.
- Appreciating and marvelling at the vast array of different species and how this biodiversity helps to keep the environment, and everything living in it, healthy.

2 VOCABULARY

Story vocabulary

Pack	—	*family of wolves*
Den	—	*a hole in the ground where wolves live*
Shepherds	—	*people who look after flocks of sheep*
Coax	—	*encourage*
Crevices	—	*cracks in rocks*
Inexperienced	—	*without experience*
Descended	—	*went down*

Associated environmental vocabulary

Anthropogenic	—	*human caused*
Extinction	—	*dying out of species*
Habitat destruction	—	*the complete ruin of specific areas such as forests, woodlands, mountain pastures, etc.*
Co-existence	—	*living alongside each other*

Continued . . .

Making Friends

Making Friends

Hanni crawled into the hole that had been dug out under the rocks. The low whimpering sounds he had heard suddenly stopped. He inched his way slowly forward until his hand touched soft fur. The wolf pup was frightened and trembling. "It's OK", said Hanni softly. "Don't worry. You're going to be fine." Hanni thought it was very odd that the pup was all alone. Where was the rest of the pack? he wondered, knowing that wolves lived in family groups. The pup whimpered again. It was a sad sound and Hanni wanted to protect it. Can I succeed? he thought to himself.

Back outside the hole, Hanni placed a piece of ham from his lunch on the ground, and hid behind a rock close by. Soon, the wolf pup came out of the den, and looked around nervously in the brightness of the daylight. Crouching low to the ground, the pup made its way towards the food and gobbled it down quickly before disappearing again into the den.

Hanni was patient. He was spending two weeks in the mountains with his father and two of the shepherds so he had plenty of time to try and coax the young wolf out of the den.

Taking the sheep to the high pastures was something that was done every year in the summer when the sun was at its hottest. Up here the air was cooler and the grass sweeter for the sheep to eat. Erul and Giorgi, the two most experienced guarding dogs, were with them to protect the flocks from wolves and bears. Now, the two dogs sat under the shade of a large boulder out of the sun, keeping a watchful eye on the sheep.

Hanni was at home in the mountains. For most of his nine years, he had scampered over the rocks and boulders that covered the hills and slopes of the mountain, looking for the bright green and turquoise sand lizards and wild tortoises. The lizards were quick and the slightest movement sent them darting into cracks and crevices in the rocks.

In the early evening, Hanni returned to the wolf den. There was no sign of the pup and no sign of any adult wolves. He carefully placed some more meat outside the den and then went back to the camp to have supper. The sheep had been rounded up for the night and huddled together. The dogs huddled with them, curled up, and sleeping, but always alert for danger. Hanni sat with his father by the campfire and soon they started talking about the wolves that had been seen in the area. The shepherds told his father about two wolves that had been shot by hunters last week after they had killed some sheep from another flock. Hanni was upset by this news, and felt sure that these were the pup's parents. As soon as it was light in the morning he would go to check the den again.

The sun rose slowly behind the mountain. It was still chilly. Hanni wrapped himself in his warm coat, put three large pieces of meat in his pocket, and set off to find the pup. It took him ten minutes to reach the den. The meat he had left the night before had gone. He hoped that the wolf had eaten it. The den was silent. Hanni placed one of the pieces of meat on the ground outside the den and another piece a few feet away. He hid behind a rock and waited.

After a while, a small brown head with a shiny black nose popped out of the den. The pup was still frightened but he quickly ate the first piece of meat. He looked at the second piece of meat hungrily. Hanni came out from behind his rock, moving very slowly and carefully. He crawled towards the wolf on his hands and knees, and gently called to the wolf. The pup raised its head, but it didn't run away. Hanni moved towards it, talking to it as he went. He held out the last piece of meat. The pup was more hungry than it was frightened and stood still, sniffing the air, while Hanni approached it. Hanni could now see that the pup was a male wolf. Before he went to sleep last night, Hanni had thought of names for a boy wolf and a girl wolf.

"Vucho, here boy", he said softly. The pup looked at him and cocked his head on one side. "Vucho", said Hanni again. "Here's some more meat. Good boy. Good boy. Everything's fine. Good boy."

Now he was close enough to touch Vucho. His fur was soft and warm, but at the same time there were lots of tough, wiry hairs. His coat had many different colours. Behind his ears the fur was almost orange, and on his back there were black hairs, white hairs and blonde hairs. There was a black tip on the end of his long tail.

Vucho took the meat from Hanni's hand, and ate it quickly. Still he didn't run away. Hanni sat still, and after a while Vucho lay down next to him. The boy and the wolf stayed like this for some time, happy in each other's company.

Soon Hanni heard his father whistle to the dogs. He got up. "Vucho," he said. "I have to go now, but I will be back later, and I will bring you some more food." There was still no sign of adult wolves. There were no fresh paw prints around the den, and Hanni was sure Vucho had been on his own for a few days.

By the end of the week, Hanni had visited the den every morning, lunchtime and evening. He shared his food with Vucho and it wasn't long before Vucho trusted him enough to play. The two of them played hide and seek behind the rocks and boulders, and they ran through the mountain streams.

As the two weeks started to come to an end, Hanni worried about how the young pup would survive. There had been no sign of other wolves and Vucho was still too young and inexperienced to hunt for himself. He could catch smaller animals, but this would not be enough.

On the last night at the camp, Hanni lay awake. In the far distance he heard a wolf howl, but it could have been the wind. It was a long time before he got to sleep, and the last morning came around very quickly. Hanni grabbed as much meat as he could and some pieces of cheese and bread. At least Vucho would have something to eat for today and possibly tomorrow. He had succeeded in protecting the young wolf so far, but what else could he do now? Soon he would have to go home, and Vucho would be left to fend for himself.

When he got to the den, it was empty. Hanni was very worried. Where was Vucho? He had been there every morning waiting for Hanni to bring him food. He sat down and waited for a while, but by mid-morning there was still no sign of Vucho and it was time for him to go. His father called to him to hurry up. With a heavy heart, Hanni left the den. He put all the food inside the den and hoped that Vucho would be back to eat it.

"Hanni, why are you so sad?" his father asked as they made their way back down the mountain. Hanni told his father it was because he didn't want to go back home just yet and he enjoyed being near wild crea-tures. He had had such a great time taking the sheep to the high pasture. His father nodded. He understood.

A little while later, Erul, the eldest dog came over and nuzzled Hanni's hand, and gave a short bark, before running off. This was very unusual. Hanni had grown up with Erul and he had never behaved like this before. What could it mean? Suddenly he heard a noise over the ridge, a series of barks and yips, and a short howl. Hanni stopped and looked up at the ridge. There were rocks everywhere, and he looked at each one, checking for any sign of movement. Every rock looked like a wolf sleeping. His eye caught a movement at the top of a ridge, and he could see what looked like two pointed ears. A head appeared, and there was Vucho. Hanni's heart raced. And then to the left of Vucho another head appeared. A much larger head. The two wolves watched as the shep-herds and their flocks descended the mountain. Only Hanni knew the wolves were there. He hung back and let the sheep and dogs carry on down the slope. The adults were busy talking to one another and paid no attention to Hanni. He looked over towards the ridge. The wolves stood and watched him. Vucho barked twice and disappeared behind a rock. The adult wolf followed him. Perhaps the older wolf was his brother or sister from last year and had come back to rescue him, thought Hanni.

They slept one more night on the mountain. Hanni lay awake again. In the distance he heard two wolves howling. They were calling to each other, getting ready to go hunting. He smiled. He had succeeded in keeping Vucho safe for the past two weeks, and now the older wolf had taken over. Vucho had a family again and someone to look after him. Hanni snuggled down in his thick, warm blanket, and went to sleep and dreamt about meeting Vucho again next summer.

4 TALKING ABOUT THE STORY

- Why was the wolf pup frightened and trembling?
- Why were Hanni and his father in the mountains with the shepherds?
- Why did Hanni want to protect the wolf pup?
- What other creatures did Hanni meet on the mountain?
- Where did the wolf pup live?
- Why were the sheep taken to the high pastures?
- What news upset Hanni and why?
- How did Hanni make friends with Vucho?
- What food did Hanni bring for Vucho? What do wolves usually eat?
- Why was Hanni worried about Vucho being able to survive on his own?
- Who rescued Vucho at the end of the story?

Points for discussion

- Wolves live in family groups called packs. Discuss this with the children.
- The story is based on a real project in Bulgaria that helps to conserve large carnivores. There is still a problem with wolves being hunted in Bulgaria. Discuss the hunting of large animals with the children and the different types of hunting, including subsistence hunting, trophy or sports hunting, wildlife population controls.
- Humans are encroaching increasingly on wilderness areas which brings human societies into conflict with different species of animals, particularly the larger species such as wolves, bears, elephants, tigers, and lions. Learning to co-exist with larger species is important for their future survival. Destroying natural habitats means that many large species have less space to move around and to build their homes, or search for food. How can we protect natural habitats from destruction? What can we do to protect the different species? What can we do to conserve indigenous human cultures?

5 LEARNING ACTIVITIES

Appreciation

In the story, Hanni loved watching wild creatures in their habitats and was careful not to hurt them. This is how he observes lizards and amphibians:

Suddenly something caught Hanni's eye. A lizard sat a few feet away from him, sunning itself on a rock. Its bright green and turquoise scales made a beautiful pattern all over its body. Being as quiet as possible, Hanni moved towards the lizard. When he was close enough to touch it, he quickly grabbed it around the middle, and then cupped the lizard in his hands so it could not escape. Hanni had patiently learned how to catch them without hurting them. He knew that if he caught a lizard by its tail, the tail would break off. He took the lizard back to the camp which his father and the shepherds had set up for their stay, and carefully placed it in a bucket. Inside the bucket there was a frog and two toads. Hanni had placed some water in the bucket, some plants and two large rocks. He liked to look at the amphibians for a while before letting them go again.

Ask the children to write a paragraph about a creature they have closely observed without frightening or harming it. This could be a real experience or they could make one up. (Younger children could draw a series of pictures depicting this experience of interacting with a wild creature.)

Conservation

The conservation of wildlife habitats and the biodiversity of species is of international concern. The world's ecosystems need to be healthy to support the vast array of life. Land masses and continents comprise many different countries, with different human cultures and a variety of flora and fauna. To conserve the biodiversity of our planet we need to understand how ecosystems work, and what we can do as citizens of the world to help keep them healthy.

Many creatures do not recognise human and political boundaries, and there are numerous species that migrate over great distances. Using the internet for research, and as an example, you could tell the children a short story about the migration of the caribou across the frozen tundra to their calving grounds and how they have to find food to eat, while at the same time staying out of harm's way from large predators such as wolves and bears.

Working in pairs, ask the children to select a migrating animal: a bird, or a large mammal, or perhaps migrating salmon. They can then create a story, poem or series of pictures about the animals' journey, the perils they face, and the different creatures they meet along the way.

Protection and enhancement

There are many conservation organisations throughout the world that are working to protect and conserve ecosystems and habitats, different species and the biodiversity. It is also important to protect and conserve indigenous human cultures and societies in different countries.

Using the IT suite and the school library, ask the children to research conservation organisations in the UK and in different countries. Many of these organisations have websites with lots of information and resources.

An example of an interactive website is the International Wolf Center website (www.wolf.org). The children can use this website to track radio-collared wolves in America.

Other websites have webcams so that the visitors to the site can watch the daily lives and activities of a range of fascinating creatures. It is easy to find webcam projects on the internet using a simple search.

Picture activity

Give each child a photocopy of the picture provided. Use this as a springboard into creative writing – a poem, a description or story. And/or for a research project, using the school library, the bulk library loan and IT suite, how much can the children find out about wolves and/or juniper trees?

Additional learning activities

Exploring the world through the eyes of visitors

The world is made up of many different animal and human communities. In small groups, the children can take turns to play the role of a journalist or reporter, a migrating person from a far away country, and a migrating animal from a far away country.

Using source materials such as photographs, books, maps and other documents, the children can research their chosen subject to provide background information.

Next, the children playing the role of the journalist can interview the migrating person and the animal. Give the children some guidance in interview techniques such as using open questions (who, what, why, when, where, how). The aim is to uncover interesting facts and information that give different perspectives.

The children playing the role of the migrating person or animal can choose a few different facts about their experiences in a different country and what life is like there.

If time allows, let each child have an opportunity to play the different roles.

Once the exercise has been completed, the teacher can hold a whole-class discussion about what has been discovered. What problems did the person or animal face in their own country? How is it different from life in the UK? What dangers did they face making the migratory journey? Who helped them along the way?

Predator and prey role play

The children will role play deer and wolves to re-enact the predator/prey relationship between two species.

Background information
Deer are one of the primary prey species for wolves. The wolf populations vary depending on available prey.

Wolves are often killed by large prey species as they have powerful hooves and sharp horns.

Activity – the deer and the wolf
Time required for activity – one 45 minute lesson to explain the activity and rules, take the children outdoors, and time to discuss what the children observed.

Rules of the activity
- Each student will wear a colour paper tag tied with string. The deer will be given a 30 second head start to run to safety zones.
- Every minute for each of the 20 minutes, a wolf is to be removed from the game by the teacher as it is lost to starvation.
- Safe zones for deer are lakes, forests, mountains. Deer can remain in these for only 3 minutes to feed and rest. If they stay beyond three minutes, one deer will die from starvation.
- Each wolf and deer will try to pull the colour paper tag from each other, representing a kill of the other species. They are then taken from the game until the 20 minute period has ended.

- Deer must behave as prey and run from the wolves, except when trapped when they may try to pull the colour tag from wolves. They may rest and feed in the safe zones.
- Wolves must behave as predators and chase deer from zone to zone, trying to pull colour tags from them.
- At the end of the 20 minute period, return to the classroom.

Procedure

Divide the class into mixed groups. There will be more deer than wolves. Mark out the safe zones. Discuss the rules as above. Hand out the colour paper tags which the children attach to themselves. Conduct the activity for 20 minutes.

Assess how many of each species survived, and discuss reasons for the survival rates of each species.

PICTURE ACTIVITY

© Mal Leicester, Denise Taylor, Routledge 2009

Photocopiable
Resource
PICTURE ACTIVITY

Countries Far Away

Theme: Protecting and enjoying wildlife habitats and biodiversity in countries far away

Introduction

The assembly leader introduces the theme and talks about our wonder and awe at creation and the beauty of the natural world and why we should look after natural habitats and the many different species that live in them.

Story

The assembly leader says:

This is a story about a boy and a wolf in Bulgaria. The little boy, Hanni, lives in the mountains with his family. In rural Bulgaria, sheep are kept in flocks with shepherds and livestock-guarding dogs looking after them to protect them from large predators such as wolves and bears.

Song

Select a suitable song or hymn. For example:

The World is Such a Lovely Place
No. 8 in *Every Colour Under the Sun* (Ward Lock Educational Co Ltd, 1983)

Who Built the Ark
In *Someone's Singing, Lord* (A&C Black)

This is a Lovely World
In *Someone's Singing, Lord* (A&C Black)

Poem

Select a suitable poem. For example:

The World by William Brighty Rands
In *Treasury of Poetry & Rhymes* (Parragon)

Don't Bring the Camels in the Classroom by Kenn Nesbitt
In *The Aliens have landed at our school* (Meadowbrook Press)

The Rime of the Ancient Mariner by Samuel Taylor Coleridge (widely available)

Quiet reflection or prayer

For a universal, humanistic or multi-faith assembly:

The assembly leader says:
Think of countries far away and the many different types of plants and animals that live there (pause). Wonderful creatures such as tigers, lions, bears and wolves live in forests, mountains and prairies (pause). Think about how we can help to protect and conserve creatures and habitats in other countries (pause). Think about how we can help our neighbours in other countries to live alongside the different species of animals.

Or for Christian schools:

Let us pray.

God the creator,

Thank you for the many wonders of the world in countries far away; the variety of plants and animals that share our planet. Help us, Lord, to protect all the creatures and animals, and to help our neighbours in other countries to live alongside them.

Amen.

CHAPTER 8

The Planet

Theme Eight: The Planet: the global issues

We must appreciate, conserve and enhance our fragile earth. We must understand what each of us can do to help to protect the planet.

Environmental Values

- Appreciation: understanding that the Earth is a living organism. Understanding the Gaia theory.
- Conservation: to value biodiversity and learn about endangered species.
- Protection and enhancement: to contribute to preventing pollution to air, water and land, both to keep a clean planet, and as part of preventing global warming.

A Suggested Lesson Plan

1 Introduce the theme

We need to introduce the children to the more global issues associated with environmental education concerning looking after Planet Earth.

2 Vocabulary

The teacher ensures that the children understand the words given.

3 The story

The teacher shows the illustration and reads the story.

4 **Talking about the story**

The teacher uses some of the questions and discussion points given, stimulating the children to talk about the story/theme.

5 **Learning activities**

The story and associated activities encourage listening and discussion skills. Follow-up activities introduce environmental education at a more global level encouraging appreciation of the interdependence of people, creatures, plants, land, sea, air and sky.

1 INTRODUCE THE THEME

It is said that even the fluttering of a butterfly's wings in one part of the world can affect the environment in another! This is because everything is related to everything else.

The Gaia Theory: James Lovelock believed that we must think of the world as an interdependent mix of systems and cycles and he called this totality of interaction – Gaia.

2 VOCABULARY

Story vocabulary

Fragments	–	*small pieces of something broken*
Desperate	–	*hopeless, despairing, reckless out of despair*
Deposit	–	*place; lay*
Ached	–	*hurt*
Rare	–	*scarce*
Starve	–	*ill-nourished; without food*
Extinct	–	*no longer existing, wiped out*
Neighbouring	–	*nearby*
Weary	–	*tired*
Exhausted	–	*very tired*
Terror	–	*fear*
Fragile	–	*easily broken, delicate*
Shred	–	*tear up*
Plummet	–	*drop sharply*
Sodden	–	*wet through*
Harbour	–	*safe mooring for boats*
Offspring	–	*your child or children*
Pride	–	*pleasure at something worthily done*
Glittered	–	*sparkled with light*

Associated environmental vocabulary

Global warming — *the warming up of the Earth because the atmosphere is polluted*

Carbon footprint — *the amount of carbon gases produced by a process, person or machine*

Fragile Earth — *the vulnerability of Earth and its life-forms due to pollution and the destruction of natural resources*

Greenhouse gases — *the gases that trap the sun's heat to produce global warming*

Eco disaster — *a disaster to humans or other creatures caused by damage to the environment*

Climate change — *changes in temperature and weather patterns due to global warming*

Weather systems — *the patterns and processes that produce different weather in different places at different times*

Blue Planet — *the Earth is known as the Blue Planet because 70% of the surface is covered by ocean. When viewed from outer space the Earth looks blue because of these oceans*

Continued . . .

Fragments of Fallen Sky

Fragments of Fallen Sky

The rounded wings of Sand Island's lost butterflies are vivid blue, patterned with cloudy white swirls. Once they used to bask on the island's pale beaches, fragments of fallen sky.

Epica flew over every inch of Sand Island, desperate to find a Tay Plant on which to deposit her eggs. Her wings ached and at last she came to rest on a small leafy tree. She found herself looking down on a young girl and boy.

"Look," said the girl, pointing up at Epica. "A Blue Sand butterfly!"

"Wow," said the boy. "I've never seen one before."

"They're very rare now. We've cut down all the Tay Plants and their caterpillars starve."

"There are Tay Plants on Little Sand."

"Yes, but Blue Sand butterflies live only here. Unless one of the few that remain gets blown over to Little Sand, the Blue Sand butterfly will soon be extinct."

Epica listened to all of this with dismay. Although Little Sand was the neighbouring island, it was several miles away over the sea. *But I have no choice*, she thought. *Unless I reach Little Sand, my caterpillars will starve.*

Epica flew out of the tree and headed to the beach. Below her she saw turquoise waves and the deeper, darker, endless blue sea beyond. A big shudder rippled across her wings. She didn't want to leave her own Sand Island, and she wasn't sure she could find the way, but she knew she must try. She took a deep breath and flew on, and on and on and on and on. Her wings were weary, but there was no place to rest.

By the time it began to rain, Epica was already completely exhausted. Her aching wings grew even heavier with water and water poured into her eyes. Inside too she felt drowned in terror. Either the rain would shred her fragile wings or the increasing cold would freeze them to a stop. She would plummet into the sea and be smashed.

I'm not going to make it, she thought. Just then, blurred by the rain, Epica saw yellow lights far beneath her. *Could that be a ship*, she wondered. She flew downwards, nearer to the terrifying ocean.

It was a ship! Hope washed away Epica's fear. She landed on the deck thoroughly soaked and only just before her sodden wings finally collapsed. She crawled into a quiet, sheltered spot and waited there to dry and to warm. And eventually when the ship sailed into harbour, Epica fluttered her dry wings to test them and was able to fly away, onto the island.

By this time it was dusk, and Epica rested on the island's vegetation until the morning sun shone down, dappling the leaves that sheltered her. Epica could hardly believe what she saw. She was surrounded by the luxurious, distinctive, grey-blue leaves of the beautiful Tay. She had made it!

Epica felt a swell of joy, big as the waves of the ocean over which she had journeyed. Here Epica could deposit her eggs and when they changed into caterpillars they would eat and eat until they were plump. Eventually they would turn into beautiful butterflies and lay down eggs of their own. Little Sand would be the new home of Sand Island's lost fragments of sky. Epica had saved her own offspring, and in so doing had saved the Blue Sand butterfly for the world. Tears of pride glittered in her eyes.

4 TALKING ABOUT THE STORY

- Why did the Blue Sand butterflies look like fragments of fallen sky?
- Why were the Blue Sand butterflies becoming extinct?
- Why did Epica think that she wasn't going to make it to Little Sand?
- How did Epica save the Blue Sand butterfly for the world?

Points for discussion

- Why should we care about Epica being the last Blue Sand butterfly? (Think about biodiversity and the extinction of species.)
- If you read *The Last Water-Zeddar* (see photocopiable page) to the children, you can compare the two stories, and discuss:
    - Why do Omega and Iona think that they are the last of their kind?
    - What type of creature do you think Omega is?
    - Who was hunting Omega, and why? (Think about the food chains and the difference between hunting for food and hunting for sport.)

5 LEARNING ACTIVITIES

Appreciation

Butterfly lifecycle

Give each child an A4 piece of thin white card. The children divide this into four squares. In square one each child draws eggs on a leaf. In square two they draw a larva. In square three, a caterpillar and in square four a beautiful butterfly. At the top of the sheet they can print the words, "The Butterfly Lifecycle".

Conservation

Invite a visiting speaker from a local conservation organisation to talk about the work of their organisation, to answer the children's questions and to discuss with them what we can do to help meet the conservation aims of that organisation.

Before the speaker's visit, give each child a copy of the photocopiable page, and read this page together. For younger children, it will be too difficult to understand the concepts. Therefore, if you digest the information, you can convey this at the appropriate level.

Protection and enhancement

Give the children the photocopiable page. Using the bulk library loan, school library and IT suite they should choose and research one of the endangered species. The children come back to the class and take turns to read out what they have discovered. They could also write their own extinction story and discuss what we could do to help in relation to endangered species.

Note: Inform the children that not all kinds of the creature they choose may be endangered. When they research the creature, they must focus on one of the kinds of that creature which is endangered. For example, wolves are not endangered as a species, but sub-species of wolves are, such as the Ethiopian Wolf or the Red Wolf.

Younger children could choose one of the endangered species – a creature they already know perhaps – and paint a picture.

Picture activity

Give each child a photocopy of the picture provided. Use this as a springboard into creative writing: a poem, description or story. And/or for a research project, using the school library, the bulk library loan and IT suite, how much can the children find out about bears and/or the forest?

Additional activities

- **The Last Water–Zeddar** (photocopiable pages)
  Read and discuss *The Last Water-Zeddar*. Compare and contrast *The Last Water-Zeddar* with the story *Fragments of Fallen Sky*.
- **Wildlife documentary**
  Show the children one of the TV documentary episodes of Life on Earth or Planet Earth and discuss this with them
- **Symmetrical butterfly picture**
  Give each child a piece of white card. They fold this in half and cut out half a butterfly shape. This opens to make a complete butterfly. On one side of the fold they add blobs and thick streaks of different coloured paints. Refold the card and press down. Open again to find a symmetrical coloured butterfly. These could be glued on to a large blue sheet of paper for a colourful classroom display.
- **Conservation poem**
  Give each child the photocopiable page. Having read this together, the children can do their own one-word message. Older children, in addition, can write their own simple poem.
- **Classroom display**
  Having completed the work of all eight chapters, let the children help you to select work from each of the eight environmental topics, and mount these for a complete classroom (and/or assembly) environmental display. Select work on homes, gardens, the built environment, green spaces, the countryside, the seaside, countries far away, and Planet Earth. Include written work and pictures.

It would take this whole book many times over to list all the endangered species. Those on this page are only a small selection. Reasons for endangerment/extinction include: catastrophe (e.g. the meteors and dinosaurs), hunting, pollution (chemical and atmospheric), habitat destruction (e.g. destruction of forests and marine environments).

MAMMALS	BIRDS	REPTILES AND AMPHIBIANS	FISH	INVERTEBRATES
Whales	Sparrowhawk	Alligator	Catfish	Spiders
Barbary sheep	Lark	Toads	Rainbow fish	Centipedes
Wild yaks	Kingfisher	Turtles	Seahorse	Amphipods
Giant panda	Woodpecker	Crocodiles	Lamprey	Shrimps
Chimpanzees	Swift	Geckos	Sand tiger shark	Crayfish
Wild dogs	Kiwi	Ghost frog	White shark	Beetles
Gorilla	Heron	Tree frog	Dusky shark	Butterflies
Otters	Stork	Iguana	Stingray	Dragonflies
Flying lemur	Cuckoo	Giant lizard	Swordfish	Velvet worms
Giant armadillo	Albatross	Tortoise	Sturgeon	Mussels
Dolphins	Flamingo	Blind snake	Bony tail fish	Clams
Porcupines	Antbird	Komodo dragon	Chubb	Snails
Zebras	Linnet	Adder	Halibut	Sea anemone
Cheetahs	Jacamar		Cod	
Lynx	Crane		Flounder	
Snow leopard	Penguin			
Mongoose	Storm petrel			

INFORMATION PAGE

Global warming

Some of the gases produced by industry, central heating in our homes and motor vehicles rise up in the atmosphere and trap the sun's heat in what is called the Greenhouse Effect. This will result in global warming – melting ice caps to cause massive flooding, and destroying habitats causing massive extinction.

Chemical pollution

Our food is contaminated with pesticides and chemicals. Large quantities of these run off into rivers and accumulate in the soil. Huge amounts of pollutants are being pumped directly into rivers, seas, and the atmosphere. Oil slicks cause serious mortalities to sea mammals, fish and birds. Fishing nets drift in the oceans and ensnare and drown fish, seabirds, seals, dolphins and turtles.

Forest destruction

Paper production continues to increase. Thirty million acres of forest were cleared each year in the early 1990s. The case for conservation:

- plants and animals enhance the world
- human survival depends on a healthy global ecosystem
- when resources become depleted, starvation and epidemics increase and catastrophes escalate. For example, millions of people have been affected by major floods during the 1980s and 1990s.

What can we do?

- captive breeding in zoos and botanic gardens
- maintenance of species in the wild – e.g. full protection of rain forests
- international agreements about limiting carbon gas emissions

What can you do?

- join one of the environmental pressure groups or wildlife conservation societies
- help with small scale nature reserves
- write to your MP about environmental issues

A. Choose a short word connected with the environment. For example, CONSERVE, PROTECT, ENHANCE, NATURE, APPRECIATE.

Use each letter of the word you choose to make a one-word message/poem. For example, for the word **enhance** we could make this message.

**Enjoy
Nature.
Holistic
Amazing
Nature.
Conserve,
Enjoy.**

B. Choose another word and use each letter as the start of a line in a nature poem. For example, for the word **nature**, we could write a nature poem such as this:

Never hurt nature's animals and plants.
Always, conserve, protect and enhance.
Take a walk and appreciate the world.
Unless we mend our ways, we will
Ruin our fragile Earth and
End our living days.

The Last Water-Zeddar

Omega and his mother were the only two Water-Zeddars living by the river and one dreadful day, Omega's mother died. Omega's dolphin-like smile turned down, his sleek brown fur lost its shine and as the sad weeks went by he longed for someone to swim with, to catch and eat a fish with and just to be with some of the time.

Omega often remembered something his mother had once told him: "When you grow up, you will go away and find a wife and have a baby Zeddy of your own."

He hadn't really believed her. He had thought he would live with his mother in their small den, forever. But now he was alone and lonely. Though he wasn't quite grown up yet, perhaps he should go and look for another Water-Zeddar.

Omega didn't want to leave his den or his part of the river but he needn't go far. I can always swim back, he told himself. And I'm good at hiding from Water-Zeddar eating creatures, and mother did think I should go.

After gently encouraging himself for several days, one morning Omega dived into the river, swimming with the flow of the brown water. As he swam, worries flooded into his head. Where was he going? What might happen to him? Where would he sleep?

Before long it began to rain. Heavy curtains of water hurled down into the river. It was as if the world had turned into liquid, for water was all that Omega could see.

At some point the river entered a huge forest, and when the rain stopped the dense trees looked so dark and dangerous that Omega was too scared to stop. On and on he swam, on and on and on.

At last, too weary to swim even one nose-length more, he climbed out of the river and darted under a nearby tree.

Although Omega had seen other creatures on his long journey, such as a toad, dragon flies, birds and fish, there had been no sign of a Water-Zeddar, not a single one. Now a truly terrifying thought came into his head. *Suppose there aren't any more of us left. Suppose I'm the last Water-Zeddar in the World! Suppose I have to spend the rest of my life all alone.* Tears flowed down his face and dread, heavy as water, pressed down on his heart. This was the worst fear of them all.

The grey day gradually turned to night and still Omega wept until, at last, all his tears used up, he curled up under the tree and fell into an exhausted sleep.

But not for long. High pitched barking jolted him awake and he sprang up, and dived into the water, a bare nose-length ahead of the

Zeddar-hounds who wanted to tear him to pieces. He swam under water for as long as he could, his chest hurt and as he surfaced, he was gasping for air.

The sound of the hounds was very distant now and he knew that the hunters would not enter such a deep part of the river. He stayed there for a long time and even when he dragged himself wearily from the water he knew he must stay awake and on guard.

The long night hours passed very slowly and still Omega stood rigid, listening for danger, staring into the trees, ready to dive back into the river if anything bad should leap at him out of the forest.

Eventually dawn came, daylight creeping through the branches above and Omega was relieved. I'm going back home he decided. He turned as a shaft of sunlight lit up a patch of muddy ground and, out of the corner of his eye he caught sight of . . . something. He turned back to look more closely. Very faintly, imprinted in the mud, was a trail of paw prints – prints that looked like they just might be those of a Water-Zeddar.

Omega took a deep breath, summoned up every scrap of courage he could find and plunged into the dense trees. It was dark in the forest and no birds sang.

In grassy places the paw tracks ran out, to emerge once more in the muddy ground beyond. Omega ignored his fear by keeping his thoughts on the trail ahead. He hardly dared to hope . . . but he must find out. He drank from puddles. Hunger prowled about inside him, but the puddles were empty of fish.

Omega walked many miles deeper and deeper into the formidable forest, until at last he glimpsed bright water, glinting through the trees. It was a lake, shiny as glass and in he swam.

Once more he could hear birds singing. A loud splash made him look round sharply. And there she was – a beautiful Water-Zeddar smiling at him.

"I thought I was the only one left," she whispered. Her voice was awed and his eyes shone with joy and excitement.

"Me too," said Omega.

"I'm Lona."

"I'm Omega." He caught sight of a flash of silver in the water and snatched up a fish.

"Brave Omega, to come through the forest to find me," Lona said.

Omega glowed with pleasure. He held out the fish and they feasted on it, together.

After that, Omega followed Lona along the lake to a small gap under a tree. He squeezed in after her and found himself in a huge, round, dry room. Tree roots, like glimmering ivory appeared and disappeared in the

The Story

mud floor and the perfectly round walls and domed ceiling were made of wood.

"It's the inside of the tree," Lona told him, touching the round wall. "And there's a passage down, through the hole over there, to other rooms below."

Lona and Omega lived happily together in their hidden, secret, magical tree-den. And one wonderful day Lona had a beautiful baby Zeddar. It had a pointed nose, a dolphin-like smile and deep red fur.

"She's as beautiful as you are," Omega said.

Lona smiled. She looked down at the tiny creature and licked it, very gently.

"She's perfect, and we will have more beautiful babies to care for over the years, Omega. And we have plenty of room for them all."

© Mal Leicester, Routledge 2009

We are grateful to LCP for allowing us to reproduce this story which is taken from the file: The Fragile Earth which is part of their cross-curricular files.

PICTURE ACTIVITY

PICTURE ACTIVITY

The Planet

Introduction

The assembly leader introduces the theme: why we should enjoy and protect our fragile earth.

Story

The assembly leader reminds the children that there are many endangered species. Sometimes it is because their habitat is destroyed. Today's story is about how a beautiful butterfly nearly became extinct. The leader or a child reads the story: *Fragments of Fallen Sky*.

Alternatively, the children could read one or more of their own extinction stories, or some of the information they researched about endangered species.

Songs

Select songs which are relevant to the theme or encourage the children to do so. For example:

Pollution Calypso
Page 15 in *Every Colour Under the Sun* (Ward Lock Educational Co. Ltd.)

Where Have the Seals Gone?
Page 36 in *Hallelujah* (A&C Black)

Poems

You could use some of the nature poems which were written by the children or an appropriate one from the children's poetry anthologies. For example:

Hurt No Living Thing
In *Young Puffin Book of Verse*

Wasteland
In *Poetry Plus – The World We Have Made* (Schofield and Sims)

Pollution
In *Tinderbox Assembly Book* (A&C Black)

The Butterfly
In *The Squirrel in Town* (Blackie)

Quiet reflection

Think about the dangers to our fragile Earth – about pollution and global warming (pause). Think about the many endangered species (pause). What are three things that you could do to help to conserve and protect the environment (pause). Make a commitment to be a good citizen of Planet Earth (pause).

Christian

Lord God,

You are the creator of our wonderful Planet Earth. Help us to appreciate and conserve the many wonderful plants and animals who live here with us. Help us to appreciate the beauty of the natural world – mountains, rivers, rainbows, flowers and trees. Give us the wisdom and strength to protect your creation.

Amen

Resource List

The following is a list of resources that can be used to access further information about the topics discussed throughout this book.

Books

Fiction

The Lorax (new edn, 1997) by Dr Seuss. Picture Lions. ISBN 978-0001700123

Oi! Get Off My Train by John Burningham. Red Fox. ISBN 978-0099899600

Ring of Bright Water by Gavin Maxwell. Penguin Books Ltd. ISBN 978-0140039238

Tarka the Otter by Henry Williamson. Puffin Classics. ISBN 978-0140366211

The Rule of Claw by John Brindley. Orion Children. ISBN 978-1842555873

Watership Down by Richard Adams. Puffin. ISBN 978-0140306019

Non-Fiction

Sharing Nature with Children (20th anniversary edn) by Joseph Cornell. Dawn Publications. ISBN 978-1883220730

Hands-on Nature: Information and activities for exploring the environment with children by Jenepher Lingelbach, Lisa Purcell, and Susan Sawyer. University Press of New England. ISBN 978-1584650782

Nature Smart: Awesome projects to make with mother nature's help by Gwen Diehn, Terry Krautwurst, Joe Rhatigan, Alan Anderson, Heather Smith. Main Street Press. ISBN 978-1402714351

Language Arts and Environmental Awareness: 100+ Integrated Books and Activities for Children by Patricia Roberts. Shoe String Press Inc, USA. ISBN 978-0208024275

Earth Book for Kids: Activities to help heal the environment by Linda Schwartz. Learning Works ISBN 978-0881601954

Discovering Marine Mammals: A nature activity book by Nancy Field and Sally Machlis. Dog-Eared Publications ISBN 978-0941042062

Who Eats What? Food Chains and Food Webs by Patricia Lauber and Darlene McCampbell. Topeka Bindery. ISBN 978-0785761013

Good Earth Art: Environmental art for kids (*Bright Ideas for Learning*) by MaryAnn F Kohl and Cindy Gainer. Bright Ring Publishing, US. ISBN 978-0935607017

Nature Ranger by Richard Walker. DK Children. ISBN 978-0756620691

Earth Matters: An encyclopaedia of ecology by David de Rothschild (ed.). DK Children. ISBN 978-0756634353

Grow It, Eat It by Dorling Kindersley. ISBN 978-1405328104

A Little Guide to Wild Flowers by Charlotte Voake. Eden Project Children's Books. ISBN 978-1903919118

Organisations and Websites

Action for Children's Arts	www.childrensarts.org
Arkive	www.arkive.org
Balkani Wildlife Society	www.balkani.org
BBC – Natural History	www.bbc.co.uk/sn
BirdLife International	www.birdlife.org
British Spiders	www.britishspiders.org.uk
Eden Project	www.edenproject.com
Education 4 Conservation	www.education4conservation.org
Field Studies Council	www.field-studies-council.org
Giggle Poetry	www.gigglepoetry.com
International Bee Research Association	www.ibra.org.uk
Natural History Museum	www.nhm.ac.uk
Nature Conservancy	www.nature.org
PBS	www.pbs.org/wnet/nature
Science Museum	www.sciencemuseum.org.uk
The Three Hares project	www.threehares.net
UK Wolf Conservation Trust	www.ukwolf.org
Wildlife in our Gardens	www.wildlifegardener.co.uk
Wildlife Trusts	www.wildlifetrusts.org.uk

Videos/DVDs

There are many videos and DVDs about the natural world. Encourage the children to watch wildlife documentaries on the television. Both National Geographic and the BBC have produced a range of films which are available in different media.

There is also a wealth of film resource on the Public Broadcast service (PBS) website at www.pbs.org/wnet/nature.

Artefacts

Any natural and non-poisonous materials that children can investigate and explore both within and outside the classroom environment. Items could include:

bark from trees
twigs and small branches
leaves and flowers
seeds
shells
different types of soils – sand, clay, peat, etc.
stones, rocks and pebbles – especially look for items with fossils
feathers
animal skulls and bones – although these would need to be thoroughly cleaned and
    sterilised
animal skins.

Also think about creative ways to use discarded items from home: textiles, paper, cardboard, plastics and other materials that can be used in design and technology and arts-based activities.

Local Wildlife Trusts may be able to help with some of the artefacts such as animal skins and skulls.

General resources

A large wall map for whole classroom activities
Local and school library
Wildlife Trusts – see link above, or contact your local Wildlife Trust.